D1784997

To God be the glory for this project. I want to thank my family for their support throughout the journey, my wife Marie, and our daughter Meredith. I also want to thank the entire team of Westbow Press Inc for their dedication for excellence beginning with my initial contact Deanna George for her patience answering all my questions. Chris Varquez who was my check-in coordinator (CIC) for being precise and consistent in applying the norms and regulations of Westbow to the letter. I also want to thank Bob Degroff for his hard work in putting this book together, and without forgetting Scott Crenshaw, my marketing consultant for his thoughtful, and wonderful guidance along the way. finally, I want to express my profound gratitude to all the rest of the team at Westbow Press whose names I probably would never know, but were just as much instrumental as everybody else for the success of this project from the beginning to the end. You are all awesome, thank you!

WHY GUILT .... AFTER SEX

In a World of Perfect Sexual Perversion

PIERRE FENELON

WESTBOW
PRESS®
A DIVISION OF THOMAS NELSON
& ZONDERVAN

WestBow Press books may be ordered through booksellers or by contacting:

WestBow Press
A Division of Thomas Nelson & Zondervan
1663 Liberty Drive
Bloomington, IN 47403
www.westbowpress.com
1 (866) 928-1240

Scripture taken from the King James Version of the Bible.

ISBN: 978-1-9736-2472-1 (sc)
ISBN: 978-1-9736-2473-8 (hc)
ISBN: 978-1-9736-2471-4 (e)

Library of Congress Control Number: 2018903984

Print information available on the last page.

WestBow Press rev. date: 4/23/2018

This book is dedicated in the loving memory of my grandpa
Ton me (mae)
Merrian Jeune
1912-2001

CONTENTS

PROLOGUE

Normally, throughout all generations past that have ever been of human history, the familiar words are the following: "The youths are the tomorrow's future". These words have been successfully the driving force to help shape the upbringing of the young people of every family of our society of all generations.

Certainly, even more so today, every family of this society still believes firmly those words to be true, and yet the vulgarity that is prevalent almost everywhere you turn, also the indecency, that permeates the lives of our young people, creates an atmosphere of despair whereas morality is disappearing, and is somehow a foreign word for many; the sum of all has damaged gravely the moral image of our lives within the society. For some reason, there are a few that still believe that our young people can still be the tomorrow's future regardless the lack of morality existing among them, because they believe they can still inculcate values in the mind of many, who would carry the baton of righteousness to make it so to the next generation.

We have come to a point as society, where we make morality to become the enemy of our society without realizing the lack of it, is the cause of the destruction of the same society we want to protect. We have allowed ourselves to be bombarded by many media outlets, the trend of social relativism, a doctrine that creates a platform for sexual libertine among the sexes in violating the norms by which such activity should happen fundamentally given to access in due time by the creator in marriage relationship only.

What should our goal be? It should always be to make sure we adhere to the norms that were given in order that morality should flourish where consciously we say no to the reality of moral relativism, and to empower ourselves with a no compromising stand to keep morality alive in all aspects of our lives whether inwardly, or outwardly.

Therefore, we ought to take a stand against many kinds of human activities that have a façade that seems to be socially acceptable, but morally wrong to consider in our midst, because they are in effect destructive elements to our own wellbeing in our society. Such activities are: pornography, homosexuality, bestiality, promiscuity, adultery, fornication, to name a few, and all other sexual perversions that are part of our everyday life of the society if we want to be totally free.

In this book "Why guilt .... after sex" we are going to tackle these issues in the effort to educate, to reason together, to bring light, and to encourage the implementation of morality once again within our society that seems to be almost unheard of, so that we can put aside our differences of feelings, and ideologies, but to let the voice of the one who created it all be heard today and forever.

INTRODUCTION

The words that you are about to read through the pages of this book regarding the subject of "Why guilt .... After sex?", are purposely written to help you discover how it will affect you consequently once engaged in such activity.

Many are those who innocently trapped in the devilish mindset of cosmic view of sexuality have become addict, violent, immoral, irrational, desensitize, foolish, unlovable, full of guilt, and negative. Unfortunately, sex is not what it ought to be in general in the mind of every human being in this planet, sex is what he, or she makes it to be, which results to chaos such as: venereal diseases, unwanted pregnancy, abortion, homosexuality, bestiality, unwanted single parenthood, uncontrolled demographic, divorce, remarriage, promiscuity, self-gratification, drug abuse, poverty, disorderly conduct in law and government, public officials and religious leaders' embarrassment, etc. .... No doubt that we are in position where we are today so confused, so sexually minded because sex has become the center stage of our lives of every aspect of it, even the little kids. A few years back, what once used to be known as intimate private in a delicate sense has been commercialized, advertised through different media outlets especially television. The common phrases out there are the following, you are not the boss of me, you are not my parents, you cannot tell me what to do, I am 18 yrs. old now I can do whatever I want, your time has been long gone you're outdated, get out my face nobody's perfect, and at last not the least, sex sells.

Needless to say, we're running out of time regardless where you stand on this issue, we cannot ignore it, that there is a problem, we can do better than just sit down and not being involved to bring about change for the better. What has happened to us as a country, or a society, or as individual, did not happen overnight, we've let ourselves lure by our own vulnerability to fulfill our lustful desires, to be happy so to speak, where morality is completely eradicated, and consequently we cannot escape this guilt that is in us because of the truth that stands behind "sex".

From this book, your conscience is going to be challenged to cause you to make decisions for the better, and it is my hope desire as the author of this book, the advice you'll receive will equip you to understand the veracity of the truth of sex as it were, so that you can be the best you can be, and live a guiltless life when it comes to sex.

Allow me to visit with you in the next few pages of this book, the different corridors of our lives in dealing with this topic of "sex" to have a clear picture of our moral condition. And at the same time offer an alternative that will consider to be the perfect standard by which our lives can be morally productive for the welfare of our society, and a sure future for generations to come. In the effort to do so, we will hear testimonies of many that have come before us, and many others that have different views, and their understanding regarding the topic in question. Perhaps some of them we may be encouraged by, vexed by, laughed about, or perhaps we can learn from, but no matter what we come to accept from what we will get about this topic in this book, I hope it will compel you to do your part, in bringing back morality once again in our midst.

May God give us grace to walk humbly before Him around the idea of sex, and may He continue to bless us with the help of the Holy Spirit when each time we respond obediently toward His command.

CHAPTER 1
THE SEXUALITY IS REVEALED

Traditionally, when two people are joined together, speaking of a male and a female in marriage, it is understood that in a few months, if not sooner a child will be brought unto the world by them in the family. If pregnancy does not happen in the first three months of marriage, it will eventually happen in the next five, six, seven months, and so forth. Unless the couple has decided for the first year, or so not to have children at their own discretion, then they will start to wonder there could be a medical reason for which she could not conceive. Other than that, the in-laws from the husband side, especially his mom, and dad typically will start giving the daughter in law a tough time, and even behind her back calling her by names such as: male bamboo, or PVC pipe, fishing basket, and others.[1] Those names are typically given to newlywed women in old days to express a feeling of disappointment which is not uplifting toward her, to look down on her, just to say she is barren.

Au contraire, if everything works out well in the next three months of marriage, which is, she becomes pregnant, their next amazement as a couple to discover, as well as others, will be to determine the sexuality of the child. Back in those days, it was not by choice unlike some couples would do today, not to find out the sex of the child, which they could by means of limited medical technologies at their disposal, they would have to wait till the day of the delivery to reveal unto them the child's gender.

Many are the signs that people could point out to, perhaps would assure that the child was in fact a boy, or a girl. Such signs could be as simple as the shape of the mother's belly of a mango fruit, or an oval avocado, this could be a boy and any other shapes as long as it is a rounded shape, then it is a girl.[2] You may think this is silly to even consider under such circumstance because it is irrational, but it is true except the fact of the matter is, any civilization that has ever lived since the beginning of time provides always a way, if not ways for its people, to cope with the needs of time so that they can progress, or advance together regardless the odds.

In a few moments during her last trimester, she begins to experience discomfort and pain that come with the last minutes of the pregnancy. Such pain and discomfort are not particularly the best time to welcome them, because a baby is about to come, and at the same time will be revealed to them an unbelievable mystery that none could, and cannot comprehend because of the fact the child will come out the mother's womb completely naked, the means, by which upon the arrival of the new born, the sexuality of that child will also be revealed unto them. When this moment comes, it will be unto them, and the child, the mark of identification by which they will know the child forever, and with that mark engraved in their mind they will go about their ways and make known unto others that which they have witnessed at the birth of that child whether, or not it was a boy, or a girl.

The mark of identification, of a child upon birth, gives to the ones that are called parents the authority to lead and make decisions upon the child's life throughout the time he, or she is going to spend with them. Not only they will have authority over the child's life, but also, they will have responsibility to care for this child immediately after he, or she comes to this world. Because of the child's gender, they are going to care accordingly to promote his, or her sexuality which in turn will develop a habit to the child as he, or she grows up to know what to do and what not to do with his or her life, but specifically with his or her sexuality. Therefore, as parents whatever they decide to do to impact the child's life whether inwardly, or outwardly in the upbringing of the child is of a vital importance because it will determine the mindset of the child to whoever he, or she is going to be in this society, and in all other aspects of his, or her life.

Finally, the wait has come to an end, she has already been transported in the hospital into the delivery room. After a very long six hours of labor came at last the baby, the excitement is overwhelmed among the friends and relatives that are present for the moment. "It's a girl" said the doctor, "it's a girl, she is beautiful" needless to say, all babies are beautiful, alright! As you can imagine, the anticipation has come to rest from the witnesses, not so much to welcome the new born, but strangely to discover the baby's sexuality. This behavior of ours is not likely sympathetic, but rather rooted in our being to be curious about someone's gender because we know deep inside first, it is a mystery where we cannot decipher the fabrication of one's sexuality as it comes to us, we simply must accept it. Secondly as much as we would want to, we cannot decide the outcome of a baby when it comes to sexuality. It is not a choice someone can make in any fashion or form; it is given to us to embrace primarily by the parents, and the society secondarily.

This fact of how a person was born physically is still untouchable by any groups, experts, or medical savvy to even attempt to counteract the physiology make up of a human being scientifically as it relates to gender. Certainly, there are attempts that have been made, and successfully presented in various medical textbooks and other formats, the understanding of a human gender and the functioning of each respective organ in relationship with each other as human, just like it is among animals. So, you see there is no formula that can put together a human being, or its gender for that matter outside the place where it all started the mother's womb. Even though certain experiments have been conducted over the years to make a human being via a scientific method known as "cloning" which is really in essence the replica of a human who is, or was existed, and more precisely such experiment can only be made possible through the use of a cell, or cells from that human in order to produce another.[3] The bottom line is, we can use science to help us understand for the most part, the functioning of our members, and our organs, and perhaps the use of them in our body, so that we can appreciate more the ability to do what we do on a daily basis, because the knowledge we glean from scientific avenue as it relates to our gender, or our body as a whole. But when it comes to the assembly line of a human as far as scientifically concern, it is impossible, it only can be explained scientifically what's happening in and out of a human being, and study it because the order of natural law permits only a human to be birthed not to be made.

With that in mind, I think it is fair to say that every human being on the face of this planet has an origin. The origin is the place by which we all come into being where our sexuality, or our gender has been intentionally decided for us, and more importantly who our parents would be, our race, our ethnicity, and our color precisely, and naturally. It is not a random act nor was it by accident that you've been given life. The reason for it, if you are alive today it's because you have been born at some point of time in the past where your nakedness was revealed to those who witnessed your birth where your parents, or guardians have cared for you because of their effort of you being who you are today. Truly I am speaking merely concerning of a human being who is alive and well, but not necessarily the moral and the spiritual point of view of a person which no doubt these issues are part of a human being, where people are to be taught to become such.

Meanwhile, this little girl who was a few hours ago attached to her mother is now learning to be in a sense independent from her mother, so that she can begin to experience life on her own. The process toward maturity is in fact in effect the moment the umbilical cord is separated from the mother's uterus to give way to a life that is yet to live in a different and a brand new way, because one has to live his life physically not being lived for, as it once was when attached to the mother via the umbilical cord.[4] For this reason, it is vitally important naturally that the child begins to learn how to do things in her own such as: cry, eat, play, smile, poop, pee, etc. So that she can be familiar with the functioning of her body and her surroundings. Not only that, her parents are going to start calling her by her name, and at the same time, they'll tell her, her gender as it relates to her name. These ingredients are very important to support her in the process of becoming mature which eventually will become also a second nature in her everyday life.

Later, when she becomes older, these things that have been taught to her are going to be the fuel that will help her to defend, protect, or how to engage sexually in her lifetime. Make no mistake parents, the child that you know of as a baby, very innocent not knowing what to do in his own, will eventually become a grownup child, if there is no reason for the life of the child to be cut short. That means you got to be busy installing good, and solid foundations in the child because these solid foundations are the ones that are going to help your child to survive the vicissitudes of life which can be dangerous as they relate to her sexuality.

First place to start can be to explain to the child that the life, that he, or she has, did not come from you as parents, but it was a gift and even as well as her gender, because you as parents could not able to choose her and her sexuality even if you wanted to. Once you get to teach your child, or children that you happen to be their guardian, they will have a unique perspective of who they are and how they should go about their lives in the society. Besides, they will have such an appreciation for life, they'll not abuse theirs, certainly not others, and then there will be no scenarios and chaos, where parents will not have to worry, or grieve over their children's behavior. And when all has been said and done, the child needs to know that it is appointed a day for him, or her to die, because the gift of life will be demanded back from him, or from her with no question asked, and that is the most important thing. Every one of us did not have the choice to decide our sexuality, nor who our parents and our ethnicity should be, but we can choose where we want to go before the end of our life, it is a must for everyone before death.[5]

Frankly, touching the subject of death is an incredible learning opportunity to be unlighted from, regarding the transition from life to death and after. As much as I would like to ponder greatly at it, I would rather not at this time, because the focus of our current subject is susceptible in doing more harm than good to ignore it, or to deviate to another. Moreover, death will inevitably happen to all man just like it had been for every human being to be birthed into this world. Unfortunately, parents spend tremendous times and resources to teach their children how to live, but they fail to teach them how to die. Die to self to express genuine love for others even in the toughness of time; die to the world as he/she should keep in mind that the world is a place of trouble of infamous goodness of perpetual chaos and disorder, a place of want in coveting other's worth, but die again to the devil's schemes the likes of which that destroy friendship, camaraderie, and self-esteem in keeping one from moving forward. And die eventually physically in certainty that he/she knows there is a better place that awaits ahead where at last there will be no more pain, no more sorrow, and no more death, but instead everlasting joy, peace, comfort, and love. That's what it is all about! We need to keep the main thing, the main thing which is in this instance to abide by the rules that were set before us regarding protecting the home, and the family.

Suffice it to say, that there are some preventive methods that have been in use for some to avoid having kids early within, or without the bond of marriage to defy the plan of the blessedness of life. So much so for the success of this method, that not only there are countless options to choose from to prevent birth, but also most women, if not perhaps, every woman has used once or twice these methods out there to decide <u>when to have</u> or better words <u>when to bring</u> kids into this world. These methods by which women, or perhaps some men have been using become so effective that sometimes they use them as excuses for not having children, because of financial reasons, careers, too young, lack of experience and others, but the fact remains that people in general work very hard to preserve life than to lose it, because they sincerely believe once death occurs, it is finished.

Therefore, they do not realize the way you live will determine the way you die. That is the reason why, that every parent on the face of this earth should know not only for themselves, but also for their children to teach them this awesome and irrefutable truth about sexuality which is, life is received by means of sexual relationship between a man and a woman, the same it is between a male animal and a female animal depending on how they reproduce after themselves. More explicitly, the male, both man and animal, is the seed bearer made to be planted in the womb of a female both woman and animal. Notice very carefully this figure we know of as sex, which labels a person to these two distinct genders male and female, is not simply just to identify a person sexually categorized, but rather a destined life to live on this earth which should never attempt to be altered under any pretense whatsoever.

Needless to say, that there are those who believe they can have a sex change, so that they may no longer be called by their natural names, or because they believe they are the opposite sex that is trapped in the other opposite sex, a male body to a female body vice a versa, so they have an urge to fix the problem, so that they can feel comfortable, and so forth. Well, many people who believe like that have undergone very delicate and very dangerous procedures, and many of them have been very successful both with the procedures and the deceiving, or the fooling people with their outward appearances by which people can without a doubt identify them as the gender they portray to be, but sadly they can successfully change their sexual organ, or the outward features relating to the gender, truth be told they cannot change their sexuality. It is a fact that there is no transformation that can take place within the person regarding sexuality, once born a female it is destined to live life from birth to death a female and as well as a male for that matter. Regardless of your effort to live your life otherwise against the natural, you cannot make a male body function as a female body although you can mimic it to be. It is understood that testosterone, and hormone shots can be administered to help the process of transforming a male body to work as female vice a versa for that matter, but the fact remains male is male, and so is female.

However, there are three things to keep in mind regarding where you are in this. Number one, parents should never deliberately lead their children to live a dishonest life when it comes to sexuality no matter what your preferences may be such as: do not make a boy live his life as if he were a girl, because your gender preference was a girl vice a versa. Do not confuse your preferred life with your children's life, because you've missed your opportunity. Please let them live their own life because everybody's life is unique. Number two, if somehow, you've already gone through the sex change road after discovering that you were wrong about the whole thing, please be advised do not make matter worse, accept the mistake you've made, and make it a purpose to live your life how it ought to be from the beginning and enjoy your real you. If there is a way to reverse the procedures that you underwent to, and if you can afford it as well, go for it, other than that, take care of yourself appropriately. Number three, perhaps can be the most crucial element of all of sexuality which is the guilt, if somehow it entered in the equation of your life, it can never, or will never go away from your life. From this juncture of your life, as an author I can simply suggest some ideas, or precautions with which you can decide which path to continue your life on or not, but I cannot tell you how to live your life that has been given to you the day you entered your mother's womb.[6] Remember earlier I told you that sexuality is a mystery where it is so complex that we cannot comprehend it fully. Now understand, just like life was a gift given to you at conception, which is from your mother's womb, with the intended sex as a package to you. You did not have the choice, or your parents for that matter to decide whether, or not to be a male, or a female, it was chosen for you, therefore you must live it regardless your preference, or choice over the matter. So, it is the same when it comes to make choices regarding your sexuality, your choices should be made according to the one that has made the choice for you regarding your gender, and to whom that has given your life.

The reason, or logic behind it is simply this; your sexuality is not yours, you do not own it, you are just simply a steward ready to be told what to do, and what not to do.[7] Just like a tenant renting a house from a landlord cannot in no way sell the house; it is the same you cannot do with your sexuality however you please because the principle is the same both you and the tenant do not have the ownership over a property that is not for neither of you. In fact, if you consider doing something like that which is to try to sell, or solicit any inappropriate activity with somebody else's property, you will get jailed for that, let alone with something that has far more value than a material thing such as your sexuality, how dare you to forfeit your responsibility as a steward? Often time people would say things regarding their sexuality as if there is an age period to be sexually engaged in life, so they can openly brag about it. Seriously, I think it is ridiculous and very uneducated in that matter, because it is not necessarily by an age parameter that one should have to decide when to be sexually active, but rather one should have a no compromise perfect standard to identify with where guilt is out of the question. To find such perfect standard and to prevent the guilt, one must acknowledge the principle of first time within the matrimonial boundary only, and all the time after that, because this principle leads to oneness, in other words, where two people become one solely in a man and a woman relationship.[8]

The idea that someone is such and such age, therefore he, or she can lose his/her virginity because of the age reason, I believe that someone misses the point totally, and in fact that is where the guilt comes in because there is the element of regret for the fact that someone has violated the standard that was set before him. When someone engages himself sexually outside the bond of marriage, the knowledge of stepping away from the norm brings the unsettling guilt into his conscience where he is going to learn to live with this burden for the rest of his life. This guilt could have been easily prevented if only he has learned to listen to his conscience with respect to the norms when it comes to engage sexually. First time is very critical for everyone because it's not only set precedence to our sexual life within, or without the bond of marriage, but also it speaks clearly of who we are because we become the product of what we do depending on how we particularly engage sexually. For this reason, we must make decisions based on the norms that set before us to avoid guilt and consequences that follow our wrongdoings when it comes to our sexuality. Besides, we cannot change the order of things in this world, we must learn to follow and obey them even if we should make sacrifices so that we would not have to suffer because of our disobedience.

The anticipation that it will come a time where to be sexually engaged may be the idea of everyone in general, but a few will successfully make it there within the guidelines by which it should occur. The thought of being engaged in such relationship should make you stop and think first, to wonder what it is you're getting yourself into, and to realize the fact, so that you can make a good assessment before you go to the path where you do not want to regret everything at the end. Yes, it is a beautiful thing to engage sexually with someone within the parameter of marriage, that's why it is good to have sex, other than that no good can come out of it, because the hunt of shame and guilt will soon become part of your life and cause you to continue making bad decisions. Secondly, because you have no clue of what you are getting yourself into, you are naïve, you make yourself vulnerable to some enormous potential dangers that follow your sexual behavior. Perhaps you may wonder should we be dogmatic on how and whom we engage sexually? I believe the answer is an obvious yes, because if you understand the fundamental of sexual reality, you will conclude that even though you may not follow the premise of sexual relationship as it was given to us, but you may agree that there must be norms by which we can enjoy the freedom of sexuality. To be able to say it is good to have sex means that I am not in violation with the fundamental principles of sexual engagement.

The fundamental principles are the ones we know of as moral, in other words the measure by which we can identify what is wrong and what is right. The beautiful thing about morality is we do not have to necessarily be taught to recognize morality when it appears to us. It is a built-in element in our life known as conscience which enables us to make good choices or moral choices.[1] We've never heard in the time past, or our life time that anybody who has been engaged in a sexual activity with another person publicly where it has been accepted as ok with or outside the bond of marriage. No!

Never, anyone would accept it as ok because it does not uphold the fundamental principles by which people should engage as such. Parents would not encourage their children to be sexually engaged in life however they want, or their heart's desire may be no matter how immoral they may be; they will always look for the part where they'll most likely be able to protect their children from getting hurt. Furthermore, if anybody desires to sexually engage with an object or an animal, automatically everybody will no doubt rebuke the person who has such desire, and even the thought of doing such a thing may consider to be insane by many because they believe it does not uphold the fundamental principles we all need to model from. Perhaps, you're saying what about love, should two people who love each other be not sexually engaged whenever they want to? One more time the obvious answer is in fact no! No, because love is and should not be the premise by which two people who love each other to be sexually engaged, and because love mainly, does not uphold the fundamental principles to be engaged as such, it ought to be solely and entirely within the parameter of marriage, that is the fundamental principle we must follow.

Now understand, that there are many people who do not share the idea of being dogma concerning sexual morality, but rather share the idea of being under the umbrella of sexual relativism which entails what's moral for you may not be moral for me, they just want to enjoy the sexual pleasures.[2] Certainly those who hold this view are the ones who always run to the authorities for help and protection when they are hurting from sexual abuse, divorce, molestation, and others. Earlier I mentioned that love is not and should not be the premise by which people should be sexually engaged, because the fact of the matter is first, love can be deceiving when it is only based on feeling to fulfill a certain desire at an opportune moment. Secondly, if love can be the premise by which to engage sexually, it should not be a problem or immoral when two men or two women love each other and be sexually engaged. We all know perfectly well for example, that it takes a person that is trained in aviation to be able to fly an airplane, because if a person does not apply, or obey the fundamental principles of aeronautics he/she would not be able to fly an aircraft; so is the same principle when it comes to drive an automobile. It is always required to apply the fundamental principles by which to operate a machine anything else other than the principles will result to problems, danger, and perhaps death. The principles are in place primarily for protection, and secondarily for enjoyment, that is why if we understand the seriousness of being in a plane with an untrained pilot, we can also understand the seriousness of applying the fundamental principles when it comes to sexual engagement.

It is easy to employ sexual relativism because there may not be an imminent danger to stay away from, which is probably why you proceed according to your feeling, or your desire. The danger that is presented when it comes to an untrained pilot, no one would be relative about it because at this point everyone should see how important the fundamental principles of aeronautics are, if they really value their life which I am sure they do. Well, is it good to have sex? Yes, it is if it stays within the parameter of marriage, because things are not necessarily the way they seem which means just because we have the means to do something does not mean it is ok to do. We should always make sure to know to do it the right way.

Perhaps at this time, you may be equally excited about the attraction of such wonderful note to know that it is good to have sex either by the physical enjoyment only without its consequences, or by the fact you know that it is more than the physical pleasure because of its benefits, and dangers that come with it. You know as well as I do that once engaged in such relationship with somebody, it is understood to be something special between the two of you in an intimate way, where two lives have become one, and committed to share these lives together until death due you apart.

However, being intimate with someone was not primarily intended for the enjoyment of two people, and even not two opposite sexes who love each other let alone the same sex. Because it was intended to bring two lives, or two families together to accomplish something new, or better in the eyes of the one that gives us life. By now you probably put me in a category of a person who is sexually prejudice, or maybe I am vehemently insensitive toward those who do not share the same sexual world view with me. Unfortunately, it is sad to think of me that way, I am not in any way trying to change anybody's lifestyle, or his world view, but what I am trying to do is to remind some of you how we as human beings were supposed to engage sexually the way it was intended to be from the beginning, and perhaps to educate many who have never been instructed in this area of their life how to be engaged in regard with the fundamental principles of such relationship. I do believe there is something there, that is worth preserving instead of wasting all out at our own life's expense. Because of that, I am burdened and passionate about sharing with everybody what I believe is right, so that we all can be truly, truly well and happy.

To present to you the facts of such important part of our lives is not to judge anybody's belief system, your upbringing, your desire, your background, your culture, or even your moral compass, but to encourage you as an individual to make careful decisions with your life, not because you presume they are right, but because you know they are right indeed. It is true that there is a right way to do things and there is a wrong way to do things. It is not because you are sincere about doing something that makes it right, you may be sincere with all your heart that horses can fly, but the fact of the matter is, horses don't fly because your sincerity does not change the fact, it may let you look stupid, or sound unlearned for believing that way every time you do so.

Now understand, as I mentioned it before, that our belief system, or our desire, or our world view cannot change the fact. The fact is always the fact because it remains intact just like you cannot change the fact the man who is your father even though you may call many other men dad; there is only one that is indeed your dad. If I were your medical doctor and you've come to my office for a visit, after a diagnosis of your problem and test being done, if there is a tumor located somewhere in your body, the fact is, there is a tumor even though we may not like it, or we don't want it to be, we just need to accept the fact concerning your life. Our endeavor in this life should never be to change the fact because we have a problem with it, but rather to accept it graciously and obey it every time to succeed. Many times, the very reason we face hardship in life is because we are trying to ignore the fact that is before us to deal with, and therefore we come up with excuses and options that may in some way bring relief, but until we accept to embrace the fact, we will suffer more and more for our incredulity always. For example, if a smoker desires to get rid of his smoking habit, this smoker may consider using patches or chew Nicorette gums for the rest of his life, I guarantee you he is not going to get rid of his smoking habit until he realize the fact between smoking and not smoking.

Friend, many of these examples I mention in this section may not make sense to you, or if they do, you tend to ignore them just like you've been doing with your sexuality, but there will come a day that you wish you had obeyed the fact. Perhaps, you are not there now in your life, where you are going through tough time because you know the fact, but you continue to ignore it, please don't let it be too late, where you would wish you had listened because sad things always happen when you disobey. Can everybody be sexually engaged? Yes! Absolutely, only those who are qualified which is only within the parameter of marriage at it was given to us only in that fashion. Are you married? If yes, then it is good for you to have sex, if not it is not good for you and you should not engage in such relationship, because when you are, you will be in violation with the fundamental principles of sexual relationship, and you can rest assured judgment day will come. It is a fact that you cannot escape, or change, can you handle it?

In any civilization, sexuality has always been a topic of everybody's interest, and even in our culture today you cannot talk about sex and not having everybody's attention. The question is why a topic of such genre appeals to us of great interest? The answer to that is simply "the mindset of sex in our world today" If you remember correctly from the previous sections we've talked about sex as a sign or symbol of someone's identity for both the individual and others can without a doubt recognize the essence of one's gender. Unfortunately, we do not use the sign to set boundaries by which we could protect ourselves as individuals, and others in some ways who do not share our sexual views, because of that, it seems that corrupted seeds of sexual values have been planted in fields where normally we are expected to be educated and informed, so that we can have a good stand in the society. These corrupted seeds they are planted every day in our living room through the screen of our television set, the waves of our radio, internet, telephone, magazines, and other media of information.

Not only that, we have our schools where we know our dependence for solid and accurate scientific and philosophical propagation of facts are somehow being inundated with materials which have one purpose in mind to put out of order that which once was orderly fashioned by the giver of life. On top of that there is such a thing we know as "sex education" which we normally consider to be a tool where we can find information to educate us as individuals, or a society to be able to maintain a culture of life that produces good fruits that can relate to different age groups with truth and equity.

Needless to say, that the premise by which sex education is operated is not reliable because such premise is not advocating the truth as it were in promoting when, who, how, and why to have sexual relationship, and the consequences that follow those who violate the fundamental principles of such act, not only physically, emotionally, but also eternally. The effort, behind sex education so to speak, is not to instruct with the when, the who, the how, and the why, but it is to plant the wrong kind of seeds in the minds and hearts of our society, especially our young people to implement a pluralistic view of sexual activities, which consequently will change the normal to the abnormal, the truth to the lie, and ultimately will destroy one's life in the name of education. For examples: sex education encourages the use of condoms to prevent venereal diseases which apparently seems logical and reasonable; it is a lie, not because condoms cannot prevent venereal diseases, but because sex should only take place within the realm of marriage precisely between a man and a woman. That is the norm to follow that is the fundamental principle that was given. Sex education encourages to follow your heart when it comes to sexual conduct, because if you stay protected enjoy your life; it is a lie, because when it comes to sexual conduct, we should stay away from any sexual activity that does not uphold the truth, which is not to follow our heart, but instead to obey the truth, which is sex only allowed within the marriage relationship.

Sex education can only help from a hygienic point of view, but not so much to protect you from emotional scars there are to come nor, can it protect you morally, or the guilt that awaits you after you've been messed up so badly. The so-called sex education programs that are out there are not helping the young people to have an authentic future where these programs would keep them in a trap of lies from wrong sexual information, by teaching them that they can postpone pregnancy through birth control in keeping their sexual activities secret from their parents, not only that, but also with use of condoms they are free to be sexually engaged with the person they love, and they do not have to worry about (STD) sexual transmitted diseases because both their secret and they themselves are protected. Who is in the right mind can dare say this is good education, but unfortunately that is exactly what our young people are being taught from schools of various levels of education.

Another important thing that the so-called sex education continues to push so hard, with the help of some government entities that are in place is "Sex education and sexual orientation". In the book sex, youth, and sex education, the subject is addressed to make known this fact; it says: "very little research and few articles exist that deal exclusively with sexual orientation within sex education"[1]. The author goes on to say that "Sex education can certainly address diverse sexual topics, but issues of acceptance, respect, and tolerance for this population must permeate the entire school environment" [2]. The agenda behind pushing sex education in places like schools is not tackling the core of the issue to expose the truth where students can be influenced to make the right choice, and finally implement a culture of life designed to be totally safe.

Today's world regarding sex, bring to the table such things like, gay, lesbian, bisexual, and transgender in the name of sexual orientation, which again being embraced by so-called sex education to spread the propaganda of pluralistic views of sexual conduct. For that we have a world that is so confused, troubled, and suffered from sexual disorder, which the young people have been affected by information which they received through schools, televisions, books that have been planted for some time which result this perverse mindset of sex. Now the mental state, of those who truly engage in such intentionally perverted mindset of sex of our society, is crying out for help, not in a way to repent from this philosophical entrapment to be well, but instead they want legislative protection, so that they can openly exercise their rights to create nonstop pervasive acts, without considering, not only the rights of others, but also the violation of the fundamental principles regarding sexual normalcy. For example: some organizations, that stand by the gay, lesbian, bisexual, transgender, and queer, demand to have avenues to transform schools into safe assault-free learning environments. In Rhode Island, there is a task force that recommends

- "Legislation and school policies protecting gay and lesbian students from harassment, violence, discrimination
- Training for teachers and other school personnel (on sexual orientation identity, stereotypes, and so on)
- Increased presence and access to material pertaining to gay and lesbian in schools
- Development of school support system for gay and lesbian students
- Further dialogue for students, educators, and parents to discuss issues related to homophobia and school safety" [3].

Well, speaking of these issues where schools, or places have people who are confused by their sexual behavior deserve to have protection in cases where they are being bullied, or harassed by others who dislike them. Nobody should think that it is justifiable to act insensitively toward anybody who is controversial with his/her sexuality, but at the same time it is not fair to protect irrational behavior where really, if we are being honest, that we should not condone the idea of sexual orientation to be a matter of choice to find a spot in the pie of life, but to see it as a disease that needs treatment. Consequently, we can heal those that are affected by it, and, we can uproot the seed that have been planted that brought forth these fruits.

Normally, sex education should not be an avenue of tolerance in sinking deeply in the sand of perversion when it comes to sex, but instead it should be an avenue of correctness that educates the fundamental principles to the young people especially, and the entire society. The fact of the matter is, we need guidance every once and awhile in everything we do, so that we can arrive safely and assuredly. There must be a way to educate our folks, and our young people, what is right, and what is wrong, not only on the family level, but also on the public level, where we cannot, and should not sit back and let them destroy their lives which we could have prevented.

It is often said, that it is better to prevent than to cure, so if we know this to be true, it is a matter of education, and education is there to bring light not darkness. That is why we need not to be afraid to tell it when it is wrong to be wrong, and when it is right to be right. There is such a thing as right and wrong. Right always brings truth, health, productivity, prosperity, light, character, equity, and grace, but wrong always brings lies, sickness, suffering, distress, trials, darkness, lost, and ultimately death. Shouldn't it be everyone's goal to uphold the truth, and stand by what is right, so that we can prosper, and live a peaceable life? And after all, has been said and done, we know that we have done our part to make our world better, and to leave a legacy to follow for those who will come after us. Remember the path to prosperity begins from sexuality, so does the path of destruction.

For those who obey and follow the path that was laid before them, they can see prosperity and goodness coming, but for those who choose not to obey and follow the path, no doubt they can expect to see destruction, hardship along the way, and death to come. It is only those who obey can truly be happy and successful because happiness does not come from the path you choose to take that is contrary to the norms, guidelines, or principles that were set before you, but it does come from when you choose the path that is led by the norms, guidelines, or principles that were set before you.

For the young people whether you like, or dislike those that have been placed over you as authorities, it is irrelevant, choose to obey them, and their guidelines, it does not matter whether they are your parents, if you obey them you will see prosperity and happiness, but if you don't you will suffer, and you will be in the road that leads to destruction. A fact that is certain throughout generation after generation, it is our responsibility to be sure, what it is we are passing on to the next is something of worth in the light of beauty, character, and equity. Many times, the values that are passed on can be problematic in the way they are being passed on, because they are only a matter of convenience, not necessarily authentic as to how to improve the quality of life in nature, but only to solicit a freedom of want and of choice.

For instance, it has been a sexual upheaval among the youths when Food and Drug Administration approved birth control pills in 1960.[4] The reason for it was, because it changed the tradition, or pattern for youth to follow regarding sexual engagement prematurely. The idea in mind behind this revolution was to prevent pregnancy, or reduce it among youths, but it was not to keep them from being active sexually. As a matter of fact, this idea was nothing but to encourage them more to be sexually active as they were passing along freely condoms, so that they would not have to worry about restriction from parents, or else sexual transmitted diseases.

Individual like "Hugh Hefner with his playboy empire promoted consensual sex, and the summer of love in San Francisco's Haight Asbury district brought sex, once a taboo topic, into the realm of public discussion".[5] Is this the kind of legacy we desire our kids to keep? Certainly not, but unfortunately ever since these empires such as Playboy magazines, television sitcoms, stand up comedies, deaf jam, and others like sex and the city etc. ... are in existence among our culture to entertain with the wrong kind of philosophy, and not to educate, our society will drift away more and more from decency and morality. Our world should not have to look for implementing a new program with the intent to get rid of an old program they have implemented which they believe was alright. Richard Nixon did not have to react against the drastic increase of pregnancies among the youths out of wedlock if his predecessors have paved the way in favor of morality. He had to "create a comprehensive family planning program under title X of the public health service act, and in 1972 the social security act was amended to mandate states to provide family planning services for youth considered sexually active".[6] These should not have to happen; we can learn from these mistakes and work toward improving the quality of life, not only among the youths, but within our home as well.

There is a price to pay when we do wrong, and certainly we will reap what we sow; so how can we expect our kids to be better than we, when all we want to leave for them are woes of life? They will always have to struggle to first, clean up our messes, and then try to improve the quality of their own lives, and at the same time expect them to leave a better future for others to come. No wonder why our kids today suffer all kinds of sicknesses, because they are depressed and overwhelmed at the task they will have to fulfill, that encompasses three generations at the most. Please let us not weary our kids of tomorrow with our incompetence, or even our lack of common sense that cause them to suffer the consequences of our immaturity for not acting fairly and responsibly. Parents, it is not too late to make a difference in the life of those you love for whom you have sacrificed and worked so much.

In this moment of our existence in this world, there has never been a time more pressing for those of us who are parents, or educators of some form to be more involved in protecting our family from the avalanche of the mass media in respect of sex education. Friends, the mass media should not, and I mean by any means be the primary educators of your home especially for such topic like sex. The media has a primary goal, to pass along information that is not necessarily credible, or suitable for your family wellbeing. If they get good ratings and paid for the work they have done, they can be careless about the impact of the information they send out. It is always parents' responsibility to protect their family from such industries.

Many suggest that the mass media can play a huge role in educating our young people about sex. They also believe that the media is our kids' best friends which in turn, with the friendship they can have even a bigger impact in their future. If one believes these assessments of the media to be true, it is also true that one would not have any problem to believe that the media can in fact have a profound influence on the youths in leading them in the wrong paths when it comes to sex education. Truth is told, the media does not concern itself with the outcome of its sexual lessons or promoting healthy sexuality no more than it does about selling products that bring great revenues. It is apparent that we cannot escape the appalling images of sexual references that are everywhere and every corner of our lives. It is clearly stated as individuals and as a society, where we stand that we do not strive for excellence when it comes to morality. We are rather passive than being careful in accepting everybody's expressions in the name of tolerance without investigating them, which consequently disturb our good sense of right and wrong, even in the most sensitive area where we must fight to maintain a higher standard.

For examples, look at our schools, colleges, and universities mostly in the public arena, they neglect to set standards regarding apparels in the public settings, they think that it is not their business to tell anybody to which they extend their services, what to wear, or what not to wear. They think also if they require anything else besides being students, it would be considered as invasion of privacy, therefore their goal becomes solely agents of human rights protection, instead of being agents that enforce standards, by which students should abide by, so that they too can maximize the potential of every one of them to be morally pure, and clean.

However, parents, and tax payers on the other hand, are not speaking out for the fact that, these government institutions are utilizing the resources that have been given to them for the sole reason of training and educating young men and women to become good public servants, and good citizens for the country, have failed to assume their responsibilities as they should have to, and sadly nobody is holding them accountable. Institutions and organizations that have been placed in position to control vulgarity, profanity, decency, and morality through the air waves, and media outlets, have let loose of such things because it has not been really their primary concern to prevent destructive patterns of behavior in the mind of the public, which they are called to protect and serve. Not only that, it seems it is easier for these institutions to preserve that which they supposed to destroy than to protect, even if you were to remind them of their duty, they would call you anti evolution, or anti-development.

Unfortunately, for those of us whose hearts are broken, over this libertine of indecency of our world, will find it so frustrated to watch a simple football game from the television set in our living room that some commercials are going to show without having sexual references. Not to mention, they repeatedly come up even from a stupid car commercial, where the emphasis is totally directed toward the lady in a bikini suit with an indecent posture, which characterizes a sexual attention, as if these images you have seen can make you want to purchase that car.

Ridiculously as it may sound, this intrigue of such behavior appeals to many into believing that sex appeal is the best marketing to approach potential buyers. The main power behind this unfortunate fact is in exploiting the female gender to solicit her body, to insanely draw men's attention into buying products which probably under normal circumstance they would not do. For example, this TV T-Mobile commercial which sends out many of its delegated men to persuade other men to consider subscribing T-Mobile network, these delegates were unsuccessfully contacted their targets because, every door, they knocked at, was slammed in their faces. However, at the end, the actress Catherine Zeta Jones knocked at this fellow's door to which she asked, "Do you have time for a phone make over?" and the fellow with an air of hesitation for the fact he saw a female at his door, and to see Catherine Zeta Jones at his door in person replied, "I believe I do". The point being from this scenario shows you that the men that were sent to do the same job as Catherine Zeta Jones did, did not have what it took to bring results, and it shows how stupid men are when it comes to women sexuality because it can be used to bring down men even the very most powerful ones.

With that in mind, it really tells us the condition of our mindset in the society we live in today. It is not by accident that we are gearing down toward the bottom of our existence to be destroyed, but it was well thought out purposely by those who control the means by which we live by, day by day such as food, clothing, entertainment, relationship, family, education etc. ... so that we will be whatever they want us to be, we will act however they want us to act, we will love whoever they want us to love, and follow them wherever they lead us. These facts are the diagnosis of the condition of our lives that are being controlled by a group of people who have no interest in protecting us, but to destroy us, which they carried out through philosophies of tolerance and diversity. Make no mistakes about these philosophies friends, use good judgment and wisdom as you go through this world, so that you will not stumble upon these evil philosophies, and make sure you make the right choice, even if it means to endure hardship along the way, because in the end, it will payoff for doing the right thing. Remember, there is an effective way to do things and there is a bad way to do things, make the right choice always.

CHAPTER 2

WHAT IS SEX TO YOU?

A Monday morning, I just got to work as I normally do every time I walk in the work place greeting everybody with a warm salutation and a happy face to start our day, and then I would go to my station to begin work as usual. Suddenly, I heard the footsteps of someone walking toward me from the back, as soon as I turned back to see who was coming I heard the shouting of a voice just dropped on me this unexpected information saying: "I lost my virginity". I was instantly and literally gasped at a loss for words in an awkward position as I was trying to open my mouth to say I am sorry, she cut right in and said with a delighted expression on her face "don't worry, it wasn't last night, it was when I was eighteen" then I said to her, is that right? Woo! I did not see that one coming. She went on to say as she noticed the look on my face "boy! You seem shocked, what world you're living in?" The same world you are said I, and she began telling me the story of her life, when she was eighteen, one of her dreams have come true, because she couldn't wait to turn eighteen, where she would not have to be under anybody's restriction, she would be free like everybody else to decide whatever her heart desires to do, because she would become an adult.

She was twenty-three at the time, she was telling me losing her virginity was the best thing that she could have ever done, and looking back on it she had no regrets, because she did not feel complete ever since she was younger than eighteen, she always thought something was missing, and now she is no longer a virgin, she is in a mission to let everyone know about her newfound discovery, the pleasure of being free to be sexually engaged without regrets. That may seem true to her now, but unfortunately the guilt and shame will eventually catch up with her sooner, or later, because the fact remains that she is in violation with her own body against the natural. This colleague of mine from work, for security purposes, and discretion, I will refrain myself from revealing her name, <u>believed in a lie</u> that was apparently a truth that was being broadcasting among the young people to the effect that, their sexuality was the key to their freedom in aligning themselves against the normalcy, which in turn was the expression of hate toward the authorities in their lives just as if, they wanted to say: "I hate you for keeping me pure".

However, this rebellious attitude, from their part, is a new trend that has been born to identify themselves in the twenty-first century as cycle breakers, when it comes to standard in the realm of sexuality as intended, and others as well. Therefore, to answer to the original question "What is sex to you?" is this: for this friend of mine at work, sex is <u>liberating</u>[1], it is to say it has been used as a weapon so to speak, to rupture the frontier that has existed in her life since birth between herself and the ideology of the world that says: "being a virgin after eighteen years of age is so not cool". That is the reason why she was so excited to share the news with me, because she thought that I shared the same world view as hers regarding sexuality.

Now understand that, this colleague from work is not the only one that has a different world view of what sex is, there are of course many others that have countless of views when it comes to sexuality, which they employ routinely to tackle the issue of sex in rationalizing it to their own avail moments first of all to discourage those who uphold a perfect standard, and secondly to market a culture of ideas with the intent to destabilize the foundational principles that make us who we are as individuals, as families, as nations, as it relates to sexuality. Many are those who believe, that whatever they do with their sexuality is their business, without thinking that they affect one another, because they are part of a society which contains, if I may add "People" that are solely identified by their sexuality. Unlike that co-worker who believes sex is liberating, for being enticed by her personal lusts for so long, to be even with other friends like minded, blew it off at her eighteenth birthday to be free.

There are others who believe that sex is for example: <u>fulfilling,</u> [2] that is the idea one can somewhat satisfied with the plan in mind. Another one believes sex is <u>power</u>[3] because it can be a means by which others can profit from, like pimping. Another one is <u>to gain territories,</u> [4] <u>which means</u>, every woman that a man encounters sexually, it is as if to visit a new country. Besides that, there are others who believe that sex is <u>a trap,</u>[5], because of having sex which perhaps at the beginning seemed to be an effective way to go, have found themselves in an uneasy relationship that would cost them time, money, joy, and freedom. Another sees sex as <u>a weapon</u>[6] to do battles, or <u>a tool</u>[7] to have, so that to gain control over the other party at any time, and to subdue him/her into doing biting. There are also those who believe that sex is a way of living just like any other workforce in the world because it is technically a clever way to make lots of money through prostitution, and pervasive acts from pornographic materials, magazines, etc., so they believe that everybody has <u>a useful product in the wrong hands</u>[8] if they only know how to sell it. In the same token, we have some who engage themselves in a relationship who believe they have <u>a solid link</u>[9] among themselves because they love each other for the fact that their relationship is only defined by sexual contact which they maintain on a regular basis.

Again others who believe anything else sex is, for instance, <u>sex is what water is for plants,</u>[10] that is to say, sex is the only means that keeps the relationship alive; <u>a form of payment</u>,[11] which is the attitude of mostly older women who sexually attract men to obtain favor from them; <u>sex is strictly business</u>,[12] some men and women who see sex as their workplace, they prostitute themselves to earn a living with no emotional attachment with one another; <u>another type of pleasure to enjoy</u>,[13] it is the idea that some people enjoy the beaches, or to read, to run or any other types of hobbies, so that's what sex is to them another type of hobby in the block; <u>a priceless gift</u>,[14] it is the belief of those who perhaps have been brought up in a strict conservative, or cultural background, where they view sex as something you've got to give to the most qualified one, or to give it the right moment at the right time. <u>Another level of commitment</u>,[15] it is the belief of some that have been together for a long period of time, but never have been sexually engaged, so sex to them would be as if a new chapter is introduced to their relationship which signifies the level of commitment strengthened; <u>one of the marital fulfillments</u>,[16] for some people who embrace marriage, but to keep the marriage afloat, sex has to be frequent; <u>a means of reproduction</u>,[17] it is also for those who embrace marriage union, but not necessarily strong, or current on sexual activities only if they are seeking to bring another child in the family; <u>the way by which two become one</u>,[18] it is perhaps those who have a religious background to know that sex is sacred, and it can only be performed in the context of marriage who are not necessarily advocating this belief, but believe it to be a fact; <u>the door by which life begins</u>,[19] it is the idea of some who promote abstinence around the block, because they know pregnancy can happen following any sexual relation, therefore they would use condoms on every occasion, not to prevent sexual transmitted diseases unfortunately, but pregnancies, no strings attached; <u>an opportunity to live or to die</u>,[20] this is the belief of many who think that life is too short they don't want to waste it, knowing that there are numbers of sexual transmitted diseases out there, they don't want to die as a result of falling under that category, so they want to live, that's why they would rather wait to make sure they find someone with whom they can engage with which has never been with a partner before, or has not been sexually engaged with multiple partners in the past; <u>a way to know somebody in a different level,</u>[21] this relationship perhaps can be very critical in a way to know each other, that's why it is not necessarily binding in the name of love, but rather for covenant, contract, slavery, rape, necessity, it is perhaps some come to know each other that way because of family's agreement to consolidate a debt, or to protect both sides of their assets, it is also can be the seal of a business deal between two parties or the worse of all, it can be the scar of a rape which left a vivid damaging picture in the mind, or a bitter taste that keeps one from ever loving again, and because of all these reasons which come from as a result of an intimate moment, life can be changed for better or for worse.

Needless to say, that there are tons of other opinions from people regarding what sex is to them which are not being addressed in this section only a few that has been listed, but to be fair in some way, here are some specifically five of them, two on the negative side, and three on the positive side which are going to be addressed in further details, and at the same time to bring better clarification, or understanding to each of them separately, they are:

- To gain territories
- Another type of pleasure to enjoy
- A priceless gift
- One of the marital fulfillments
- A means of reproduction

To gain territories: First, one must ask himself this question, is there such a thing as gaining territories when it comes to women? Or perhaps the better question should have been what type of territories one can gain by being sexually involved with multiple women? I think in the eyes of many, this type of behavior is viewed as promiscuous, which is by the way the fact that one does not discriminate in sexual relations at any time. It is not in any way gaining territories as it would have been in the case of a king such as Alexander the great ruler of Macedonia who went on conquering Greece, the Persian Empire, and Egypt.[22] It just only shows the perverted mind of a man and his sexual appetite for distinct types of women, in comparing them like ice cream flavors to taste from one to another, to fulfill his lustful desires. I believe a man with such regard for women is considered appalling, and insulting for the female gender, that is why most men like that find themselves in jail or murdered.

However, the territories that are being spoken of could be the fact that they have a sexual pluralistic view that the man is the dominant factor, where being able to be sexually popular in the block with no boundaries in getting the women, that's what gaining territories means because he has accomplished something of somewhat incomparable whether by force, power, money, or by charm, everybody is talking about him. Therefore, he sees himself as a character of significance in the block. Even though he must violate all the laws against sexual harassment, or even being put in the category of sex offender, it wouldn't matter to him because he has this image that he must protect of himself which gives him fame and popularity that does not come with a cheap price.

Therefore, all morality becomes relative to him, and has no regard for the laws since in his view they are arbitraries, and at the same time his effort is to rally society behind him in leading its numerous members in the path of destruction. Be careful and be vigilant especially parents who have young people that are surrounded by those who have this tendency of being the popular guys because of their athletic abilities in schools which they will not hesitate to use this arena as a tool for their interest in gaining territories in the lives of the most vulnerable young girls who long to be noticed among the pews to be popular as well. So, what's wrong with that? Can they enjoy their lives while they are young? I think the right question should be; what's right with that? Because if there is anything right with it, there ought to be all the reasons you need to make light of this trend that permeates the culture at the expense of the young people's lives and causes parents grief and the society entirely. For this reason, our young people need to pause to make good assessments of their potentials within this society to put them to good use which in turn will shape the culture for the better, where gaining territories would not equally mean destructive patterns of behavior at its best, but rather an opportunity given to the young people to redeem themselves, to make good choices in disintegrating relativism by making way for truth, character as solid foundations to build upon for a promising society of tomorrow. These are the kind of territories they should seek to gain.

Another type of pleasure to enjoy: Sex is totally fun and much more pleasurable, the reason I know that is because I am a married man myself, and not only that, but because I am also free from the guilt of having sexual relation outside the bond of marriage relationship which can be an ultimate violation of the fundamental principle regarding sexual activity. However, this is not the case when it comes to me in regard of such relation, because I have been spared from the consequences which follow my sexual involvements, the moment I decided to obey the principles which give me the green lights to be openly involved in such relation in the presence of the one who instituted the marriage relationship, in the presence of my family and her family, and also in the presence of friends and love ones who came to honor our vows and commitments to each other. Besides, this public acknowledgment speaks clearly, and sends a clear message to those who were present at our marital covenant that we are indeed in compliance with the norms and the fundamental principles of sexual relation with each other.

Well, if it is true that this is the right way to go about involving in a sexual relationship with someone, one might say that I have been involved with different people sexually, and I have been really having fun so far, so if it is only through marriage relationship that I could only find pleasure and fun, I don't need to do that, because I am not married I can still have fun anyhow, so what's the use of getting married? This is frankly an honest and legitimate question, which in any case seems to be unfair to say, it is only within the marriage relationship to be sexually involved. The reality is number one; there is no national law that says no one can be sexually involved, if it is not within the marriage relationship. Number two, if there was such a law, the majority of the people perhaps 80 to 85 % of the population would make an effort to uphold the law, not certainly because they love the law, but because they would probably fear of being punished if they get caught breaking the law, not only that, there would be anyhow a minority group of the people about 15 to 20 % of the population who would violate the law, even though they know there will be consequences if they do so, they'll do it anyway because they are by nature violators of the law.

Now understand in any form of government, institutions or organizations where there are laws, the laws are not there to make you perfect, or to make you one of the same with the laws, if you keep them, but unfortunately and sadly to say, the laws are there "To protect" most and foremost to implement accountability to everyone that finds himself under the law. Therefore, if there is privilege there ought to be responsibility, and if there is responsibility there ought to be accountability, otherwise why should one have privilege if there is no responsibility, and so forth no accountability, because without those principles life would not be worth living, chaos would be prevalent in the society, and ultimately everyone would do that which is right in his own eyes. [23] would you say this is a fair society to live in? I think for the most part, even for those who consider themselves to be the most liberal, would rather live in a society where there are privileges that lead to responsibilities that lead also to accountabilities.

With that in mind, how can someone believe that there is no accountability for his action, because for the fact he thinks he is having fun and lots of them in being sexually engaged outside the bond of marriage? It may seem that there are no consequences now, but truth be told life is like a cultivating field that is ready for plantation at any time. Once you were born, you were automatically registered to be planted in the field while you are passing through life, and the seeds, that you are going to use for the field, are your actions, your deeds, and your words, so make no mistakes friend, where there is sowing seeds there will be also a harvest sooner or later. That is the reason why "Whatsoever a man soweth, that shall he also reap".[24] Don't be a fool, thinking that you are getting a free ride. There is no such thing in life as "Free" even if it looks free it is not, because somebody must pay for it, perhaps with money, or your time, other types of payments, or ultimately your life, or someone else's life, how about that? A free stuff is always costly; there is a price to pay for something free.

So, the notion that somehow having sex is another type of pleasure to enjoy outside of marriage, by considering it to be as some type of hobby, like any other hobbies someone would have is uncalled for, because sooner, or later every one of us, who violated the law against sexual relationship involvement outside the bond of marriage, will someday pay the ultimate price, if we don't stop to get it right, we will continue to be on the path of danger of death, where there will be no hope, if we don't look for help. There is no fun, or pleasure for that matter, once the law is broken around sexual libertine.

Remember, every one of us came from a sexual vintage point. We are also the product of sexual act, and we are all a sexual entity that is capable to reproduce after itself, which is ok only within the bond of marriage, once the process is disconnected, from whence it started, the result of it cannot be productive, but destructive instead. That is why we are all responsible for our sexuality, it is up to us to keep it pure, and clean, regardless the environment around us. We all have one life to live, and when it comes to sexuality, we all have the same opportunity in this life, there is no rush, we should not be led to settle for less than for our very best, because once we open that door too soon, it may be too hard to shut it up, or never. Think carefully before you regret what you are going to do, because it is true that all the pleasures and the fun are found within the bond of marriage, not outside of it.

A priceless gift: Yes, certainly many people would agree that a gift of an excellent value would no doubt be categorized by the amount of dollars it may have cost to express appreciation, to a wonderful person in one's life. However, some may ague to say that it is not the amount of dollars that makes the gift valuable, but it is the quality of the gift, and to whom it is given to that makes the gift worthwhile. These two arguments presented are appreciated in human relationship greatly day by day, so much so that it becomes "a must" to do in any type of relationship to show appreciation to someone that you love. This is true both among rich people, and poor people, and as well as middle class families. Something of an excellent value, or meaningful is always appreciated, and is the highlight of gifts giving for a worthy cause, to keep a relationship going among ourselves as people. Therefore, when it comes to romantic relationship, it is of utmost importance, that people who love each other, who are not necessarily married, feel the need to give and to share their lives mutually in a unique way, where eventually sexual relation is automatically a given, because it is based on the desire to love one another, which they believe they are meant for each other, so what's the use of sexual restriction?

However, we find couples, who are not really abstinence's advocates, are in favor of saving themselves for marriage, and the reason for it is, simply because they believe if something's got to give, is got to be given in the right moment, to the right person at the right time, in the proper context of human romantic relationship, so that they can protect what they have invested in the relationship, both legally and socially. Perhaps you may wonder, what is so special about all this? Well, two things: number one; a person, who shares the idea to see him, or herself as a priceless gift, is a person that has come to realization that, when he/she is going to stand in the presence of friends and family, and the person whom he/she loves to vow to be with until death due them apart, he/she would be given to that one the very best of him/herself for the first time, which ultimately will bring joy and pride for the wait, even though to get there the journey has been somewhat precarious and rough.

Number two: because marriage is the arena by which two opposite sexes can enter into sexual relationship, it is ok to share each other in an intimate and romantic way without thinking violating the law of sexual engagement. Besides, it is even more satisfying to know, that both couples, who love each other, are entering this marriage covenant as virgin, knowing in their hearts, this priceless gift of giving themselves to each other, is well given to the most qualified ones with no regrets of prior sexual activities, and in fact there was no violation that could stand in their way from keeping themselves to pursue such relationship at this said moment, while fulfilling their marital bliss. That's what it means "something's got to give at the right moment at the right time".

Does it mean, if someone because of past relationship filled with sexual violations cannot experience marital bliss as equally as those who enter this relationship as virgin? Not necessarily impossible to experience this joy and pride that comes with being a virgin, if there is this willingness to start over, in finding the right track into the road that leads to marriage with a clear understanding of where you are heading to find success. But somehow, if you manage to find this joy and happiness in the marriage relationship, there is always going to be these elements of regrets, and guilt for violating the law of sexual relationship prior to marriage, because you will never know, or experience the joy to make it, if you did not break the law. You will always wonder, what it would be like, had you not broken the law of sexual relationship? Because you cannot undo what has already been done, especially in the realm of sexual behavior. That is why, it is imperative for those of you who are not sexually involved to stay pure as you can be, so that you can prevent yourselves from the pain of guilt, and regret of saying, if only I knew I would have .... Young people, you've often heard people said that "It is not too late to do well" yes, it is true, or you've also heard "If you fall you can always get up and go on" yes also true, but think about not to get it too late, or to fall mode, because that's how you are going to be successful, and to be worthy, to consider yourself a priceless gift to that special one of yours. Think about it!

A means of reproduction: It has never been different since the creation of this world, that anybody, who has ever been born, was born in a different manner, except by the means of reproduction. It has always been the product of a male person joined with a female person through the channel of sexual act, or perhaps some form of scientific method which produced a human being the same kind. Therefore, the result of this process drawn from the two opposite sexes is called "Reproduction". This term unfortunately may not be everybody's favorite to use in our circle today, because it represents more than just having a child, it encompasses the fullness of a human being of the same kind such as race. By the way, by race I mean generally humanity, which cannot be compromised, or altered by any other form of life, which in turn makes this race so unique, and important to preserve, by solely means of reproduction. Not only that, there is also ethnic group, which is based particularly on the color of one's skin, and language, to which is built a culture of life among diverse groups of ethnicities; also, we have gender integration within the race that is vitally important for the continuity of reproduction.

Furthermore, when we understand of our sexuality within our race, particularly for what purpose each one of us is uniquely different from one another in that instance, we will realize first, that we should not accept the pluralistic mindset of sexual lifestyle that welcomes homosexuality in the platform of humanity, simply because it does not embrace human reproduction by the natural means. Secondly, it does not create a haven within humanity for family as it should normally be, where STD, and other suggested sexual behavior would not be issues to deal with, and finally life would be so much simpler, and because of that, people will live longer than ever before.

You see, many people believe that the easiest way to know that two people were sexually active, it is when reproduction is about to take place, in other word when a woman is pregnant by a man. Yes, it is true when it comes to the reality of it, but remember, it does not only bring a child into this world, but it does change potentially the lives that are involved in the process for the better, or for the worse for ever, regardless the way the situation is being handled. It is being said, that for both male and female, after surviving the age of puberty, each one of them is a candidate for human reproduction.

So, with that in mind, reproduction is not a game to be playing, it is serious business, if you're being sexually active; you are in an appropriate position to reproduce after yourself. I know that I may be a little bias here, knowing the entire ramification and other alternatives that are available to prevent pregnancies, but one thing is for certain, that the principle does not change when it comes to this. It is most likely that you are going to bring children into this world every time you are sexually active especially for the male gender, because the female gender does not necessarily get pregnant each time she is sexually involved, but unlike the male gender, it is possible because he is the seed bearer, he cannot miss. Now what should we do with that? The answer is always the same, both male and female need a resolve among themselves to try to go back to the basic, the fundamental principles of sexuality. To recognize that their sexuality is not theirs to do whatever they want with it, but rather to submit themselves in a genuine way, to the principle that gives them freedom to be sexually active, only and solely, within the bond of marriage, by which they can fully enjoy the benefits that come with being compliant with such principle regarding their lives.

Then, when all the other suggested perverted lifestyles regarding sexuality within humanity are rejected, or thrown out, that's when we can really preserve humanity through natural reproduction, that's when we can have a safe society, where both male and female can really come together in a safe way to live a pure life. You might think this is wishful thinking life, some sort of an illusion anticipated life, no it is not! Please don't settle for less, but strive for your very best, so that you can accomplish your purpose in this lifetime, as you diligently follow the norms and the principles that are set before you.

IT IS NOT GOOD TO HAVE SEX

What! Ouch, are you out of your mind? In this twenty-first century mindset, you mean to tell me that "It is not good to have sex" What is the matter with you? Are you nuts? Yeah! That is exactly what I am saying. Right in the busyness of this twenty-first century, it is imperatively not good for you to have sex, unless if you are married. What does that mean? You know regardless all the other ramifications which could have been used to justify in a scary fashion, to keep you from being sexually involved, the bottom line is this, sexual relation was purposely designed for you and me only, in other words it was for a man and a woman, who are not in the same family unit, can be engaged within the bond of marriage period.[1] Now whether, or not to accept this truth, it is entirely up to you, because first of all, you are not forced to accept it as truth, secondly, it is not relative, it is absolute, because it does not matter, if you are young, or old, as long as you contradict this truth based on your preferences, or your feelings, you are also in violation against the fundamental principles of sexuality.

Perhaps you may have thought just by glimpsing over the title "It is not good to have sex" to come to conclusion that, it is clearly something that teenagers must know and understand especially of today's society, because there are a lot of risks out there that they don't know, so it would be better, if they would abstain from such activity, after all they are too young to be sexually active. In all sincerity, it would be much better for teenage boys and teenage girls not to get sexually involved right now, for the fact that they don't fully know and understand the risks that are involved for being exposed to potential deadly diseases as a result of their involvement, which probably a good advice parents would give to their teenage boys or girls, but the reality is, that is not the point "It is not good to have sex" it is rather a foundation that they can stand on, that not only protects them from being exposed to any kind of potential risks of this life, but also helps them to live a pure and clean life until they meet that special one to marry, and to live happily ever after.

Maybe you are saying there is no such thing to live happily ever after in a marriage relationship, it is a wishful thinking. I would say it is not, to live happily ever after does not mean that there will not be any problems, or difficulties along the way nor, does it mean you will be free from sickness, or death. What it means is, that you both are going to live a married life that is free from sexual garbage that have been created from previous sexual encounters of past boyfriends, or girlfriends, which may not, or may have emotional scars, or some kind residual effects of sexual abuses from other people, or other assaults that you will carry on all your life up to the grave. These are the kind of things that are not permissible for a happy, or healthy marriage relationship. Besides, this foundation, that can protect the teenagers, is also a good foundation for us adult as well, not only to protect us from potential risks out there, but also to help us live a healthy life as good example for our young people. "It is not good to have sex" is not conveying a false message, nor is it a bad marketing in our culture. It is in essence a cure to defeat the wrong implementation of sexual ideas, or teachings in our culture, that are in existence for many generations, and also it is a preventive medicine for our young people today, and generations in coming to consider, in order to keep the bad elements out from our society, in keeping the good ones in, to be able to get back to the basic ideologies, as they were to grant occasions for good to prevail over evil, for light to shine over darkness, for right to prevail over wrong, for peace over war, for love to always prevail over hate, and for life to continue to prevail over death, so that all of us can live in freedom, in liberty, and in harmony with one another. That is the idea!

What is it going to take to make this to happen? It is going to take each one of our efforts in this lifetime, an unyielding commitment to make manifest the reality of truth, when it comes to our sexuality, and not only that, but also, an unwavering devotion to clean our act of past selfish choices, as we are moving forward in the right direction for a better future. Our young people are groups of can do people, they have potentials to commit to do right, just like they know to obey the use of condoms for sexual activities as their basic knowledge, when it comes to sex taught in our society as standard, they will know to obey the path that leads to good and healthy sexual life as well, if they are taught the right kind of sex education, that should be available to them at their reach at home, school, the media, and everywhere for that matter.

No doubt about it, that it presents a greater risk to the teenagers than it does to the adults, in respect to maturity as you see we discuss it in the previous section "It is not good to have sex". Certainly, on one hand, we are not going to linger more on this idea how we've come thus far to even consider it an issue. On the other hand, however, we are going to explain in great details precisely how it affects the life of our teenage boys and girls, also the effect on their families, and the society in which they live. We do have a society of young people today that is extremely impulsive in their actions, and at the same time they are also vulnerable to commit those actions that are detrimental to their lives, and others around them. Since we know who they are as such, and how disastrous the results of their actions may be, in terms of negligence, or libertine of youthful amusement. With these clues, we as parents, or responsible adults, can offer another alternative that can rally them into a safeguard of self-protecting, or self-preserving life, which in turn will keep them safe from the danger that is yet to come around unhealthy sexual relationships out there.

Needless to remind you, that it is illegal that children under the age of eighteen to be sexually active, it is statutory rape in the court of justice with, or without the knowledge of an adult of such activity, when it is reported to the open. In the state of Florida specifically, under the Title 794.05, "unlawful sexual activity with certain miners if someone age 24, or older engages in sexual activity with someone age 16 or 17. The penalty is up to 15 years in prison; other states may vary in age, time, and degree of punishments". In accordance with the FBI definition, "statutory rape is characterized as nonforcible sexual intercourse with a person who is younger than the statutory age of consent. The actual ages for these laws vary greatly from state to state, as do the punishments for the offenders" [1]. Some other case, it is child pornography in the eyes of the law, and so it is called upon parents, guardians to be present in the life of their children as an effort to prevent those acts from happening again. Child pornography refers to images, or films also known as (child abuse images, and in some cases, writings depicting sexually explicit activities involving a child). "Ninety-four of 187 Interpol member states had laws specifically addressing child pornography as of 2008, though this does not include nations that ban all pornography. Of those 94 countries, 58 criminalized possession of child pornography regardless of intent to distribute". [2]

Unfortunately, they are continuing to happen repeatedly every day so much out of control that some laws must be put in place to seek to protect victims of such crimes which give the court the power to carry out sentences, and large amount of money as fines to predators who are sexually abusing the children. According to the Broward Sheriff's Office and Florida Statutes, "a sexual offender is a person convicted of or who has pled no contest or guilty to a sex offense involving a minor, and who is released on or after October 1, 1997 from the sanction (e.g. fine, incarceration, probation, etc.) imposed because of the offense. Offenses include, but aren't limited to, child pornography, sexual performance by a child under 18, and procuring a person under 18 for purposes of prostitution. However, a predator designation requires that a person be convicted of a first-degree felony sex crime, or two second-degree felony sex crimes (with offenses, conviction or release from court sanctions occurring within 10 years) and which occurred after October 1, 1993". In addition, the court must issue a written order finding for predator status. It is granted that such person must be sentenced to a mandatory minimum term of 25 years' imprisonment up to, and including, life imprisonment. [3]

Normally, one might say that's great in term of protecting our children, the authorities are doing their part to ensure safety for our children against those who want to harm them. Under normal circumstance authority personnel can and should exercise the law of the land in favor of a sexually abused child, but other circumstance this may not be the case where somebody is to charge for such crime. The question is, what do we do? Well, that is when another alternative should have been in play in the first place, where the law would not have to be the only means of defense that is relevant only after the act is committed. Furthermore, the law can only be effective to compensate the victims and sometimes causes more trauma by going through the process of listening to the reasoning of lawyers of things that are true, or not, and their lingo to make the predators look like more of a victim than a guilty person.

Suffice it to say, that many times a victim becomes a victim by his/her own demise regarding sexual attraction of some friendships. Which means to say, you do not have to commit the sexual act with so called "someone you love" because of your desires, or even no matter how much your feelings are drowned toward an individual. If you are sexually attracted to someone which can happen occasionally to be honest, if this individual is not in fact married yet, there is a possible opportunity that someday you may be married to this individual, but you need to socially and cordially engage this person first, right? and depending on how it goes between the two of you in this area, then maybe your relationship will lead to marriage, then your wish will also come true.

It is not a promising strategy to employ for sexual fulfillment in hoping to marry someone just because somehow you are sexually attracted to a specific individual. It can be rather disappointing to think just having this thought will lead to something serious, as a matter of fact, most of the time it never happens to make it to the altar. And if it does happen, many times the marriage relationship was just a formality to adhere to, so that you can satisfy this longing sexual attraction, and many times, when this deep feeling has been rescinded it usually leads to verbal, physical, and sexual abuse between the two because the attraction was only focused on one single element of the relationship, therefore the marriage is basically over, because it did not start on a solid foundation. That is the reason why, it is vitally important to consider the effect that sexual attraction has on our young people today amid these pluralistic views of sexual context, to participate to fit in their pews. It is more of a pressure on the young people to decide whether to go along with their pews ideologies than it is for parents to shield their children from being exposed to the risks out there.

Often time you may hear your parents say, it wasn't like that when they were young. Basically, what they are saying is, they had it better back then among their pews when it comes to sexual relation definition. Yet the reality is, the folly of sex has not been different in years past for many generations, it may have been far more different in series of sexual contexts to participate, while the exposure has been unfortunately the same in a world that is constantly trying to be better in doing wrong at the expense of its people's destruction, without giving much thought of it in this arena. Our young people most of them, because of peer pressure, find themselves in series of predicaments as they are trying to hop in different circles, just to escape consequences from either their pews, the world that shapes their mind, or their parents if somehow, they still have the fear for them again.

CHAPTER 3

SEX AND LOVE

Unfortunately, we have to consider the enormous mistake that we have made during the last century, particularly those of us at that time, who were grown enough to remember from the 80's, who could make distinction between what was sexually acceptable and what was not, when we allowed our sexual lifestyles to lead us in all kinds of erotic and sexual libertine to cause us to be inundated by this deadly virus known as HIV.[1] This particular virus, as you well know, is a sexual virus, which passes on through sexual contact from one partner to another, which also has a single agenda, that is to destroy the immune system of the body, in other word dismantle the defense mechanism that helps to protect the body against both within and without agents such as: cold, fever, airborne diseases, other viruses and so forth. Once the defensive system of the body is down, the body automatically becomes vulnerable to any critical suffering and relentless pain, which ultimately leads to death very rapidly.[2]

The result of our carelessness, or preferably a lack of regard to the principles that were set before us, brought us all to a place of potential absolute destruction of humanity I dare say, which in turn set precedence to series of destructive behaviors to the generation of the 21st century by and large they must live with, or struggle to avoid at all cost for the preservation of such race nonetheless.

Certainly, those who've been through this antagonistic fork of their lives would have thought it through if they had known they were going to face their deaths, because of this ordeal. They would probably manage to run away, or perhaps do something which consequently would keep them safe, but almost certainly they all would tell you, they've done it just for sex, or for love, depending on the fork of life they were in for the moment.

I know I may be understood as being bias on how I approach this very sensitive subject, to think that I mean to imply, that every person, that has been affected by this virus, was because of everyone own fault. Well it's got to be somebody's fault, whether directly or indirectly, someone has opened the can of worms now it seems hopeless, and irreparable. The intention here is the logic of the fact, not in any way I am trying to have an insensitive spirit to the subject, nor certainly to those who have been a victim by it, if I did come out too strong I apologize, but I have to deal with the cause of the subject, in order to better understand how to deal with it now, and also the way to protect those whom we love that are exposed to the very same virus that has brought us here in the first place. Yes! It is ironic to discover that "Sex and love" were the premises by which our friends and love ones, or perhaps because them somebody else has been declared HIV positive then, and they are still with the same premises we have today to either continue on the same destructive behavior of our sexual life, or to protect ourselves from falling into the same trap, or even better to prevent at any cost such sexual vulnerability to ever happen again from our young people, and ultimately from among the entire human race.

Now, what are "Sex and Love" got to do with this? First, you must understand like I said earlier, that almost everyone, who has been affected by this virus, or will be affected by it, would say without a doubt, it was either just for sex, or many would say they did not know; they were in love. Because of the psychological effect that this world has on our young people today, it is rather almost impossible to kind of changing the direction they are heading, even if it means, hypothetically to hurt them, they would still convince it is the right thing to do. Second, the stubbornness they cling on, thinking it is their body, they can decide to do whatever they want to with it, whenever and whoever they want to do it with, puts us in a position of no avail for a change because the reality is, it is in fact their body, they can do whatever they see fit to do with it, even no matter what they would do may cause us all to suffer. That is why I use the word world in a unique way, because it gives them such a platform which opens the door to a variety of ideas, and ideologies where one can feel totally safe to express himself as if he has the right to do so.

When living in a pluralistic mindset of a society, one can expect so much to be fighting against, as oppose so little to uphold within that society, and to be thankful for. This world, the world that every human being resides in, is a liberal world that has a vibrant message to everyone: that is "Do unto others as you would not want them to do unto you" This message is expected to be practical in our everyday activities, even among the most conservative people because it is not in this world's interest to protect morality, but instead its interest is to facilitate to everyone anything that brings a sense of happiness, whether it is good, or evil. This worldly message means that it does not matter what you do, and how it affects others, since this gives you the satisfaction you need, you may continue doing it, if you want to be happy.

In fact, this motto by which this country has been founded on, one of the phrases of the United States Declaration of Independence, and considered by some as part of one of the most well crafted, influential sentences in the history of the English language uttered by Thomas Jefferson "we held these truths to be self-evident that all men are created equal; that they are endowed by their creator with certain unalienable rights, that among these are Life, liberty, and the pursuit of happiness" makes believe that everybody deserves to be happy, because after all, that is what we all want.[3]

what is happiness? Well, in today's society happiness can be defined not by the meaning of the word as we know of, but it is being defined as the next thing you wish to have in your life, it is as if a goal set before you to attain, and you need to be motivated enough and believe on yourself that, that goal no matter what, there should be nothing stopping you, and once you reach that goal, pouch, ch, ch, ch, ch, you are happy for ever. Imagine this kind of reasoning in a society full of hopeful people that have countless of ridiculous and unrealistic goals they are pursuing to be happy.

Let's say for example, a woman whose desire all her life is to change her physical appearance into a man like, she is now in her late 40's, she has been waiting for so long because she did not want anybody to know this was her heart's desire, she also got married and had four children out of respect for her family and the legacy they had, also she did not want to disappoint her husband and her children, she kept all these to herself and suffered for so long. Now she wants to put all these reasons on the shelves and decides to do something for herself only because she wants to be happy. Her life has been a lie for so long, if she doesn't do something about it no one will, it is time to stand up for herself, otherwise she will end up dead with a broken heart, because life is too short, if she doesn't go after what she wants, no one will hand it to her, it's time to think about herself, what about her happiness? Doesn't she deserve it? The question is: can she go after what she wants? Yes! And what is wrong with her wanted to have a sex change? See, it depends on how we are looking at it, because if we are looking at it from the world's standpoint as it relates to its message, we will find out that there is absolutely nothing wrong with her wanted to have a sex change, after all it is her life, she can do whatever she wants to do with it.

In all sincerity, this is where every one of us needs to be careful on how we approach everything in life, because this is the danger when we carelessly employ the message of this world, to think that we all deserve to be happy, suggests that we have the right to go after what we want no matter the consequences. Such reasoning to pursue happiness is foolish and irresponsible, not only to oneself, but also toward others. If we seriously consider the ramification of all our acts toward others as we are seeking to please ourselves, we would not dare consider the worldly message that I just mentioned earlier, because the alternative should be the norm by which everyone should operate, in considering it for the pursuit of happiness "Do unto others as you would them to do unto you" **Matt. 7:12; Luke 6:31.**[4]

Here's another example: a friend of mine, whom I met in college, wanted to be happy. By the way, keep in mind we attended this very strong conservative college, where compromising with the fundamental principles in life was not the thing to do there. Anyway, this friend of mine, who was about 4 feet 9 inches tall, declared it to be in love with this very gorgeous 5 feet 6 inches tall blonde, which we were friends with for over a year now, was not interested to be romantically involved with him. Meanwhile, he did not act on the rejection given to him by her only to remain friends because he believed she was the one for him, except she did not know it yet. As the saying goes "Go after what you want no matter what".[5] He made it clear that he would not back down; at any cost she should be his. Even if it would take him years of waiting to be with that beautiful woman, he believed it was destiny that the two of them should be together.

This gentleman is from one of the lands of the African continent, whose accent, because of many dialects from his origin, is almost impossible to understand his English when he speaks, besides his mannerism, as a gentleman, is seriously critical in public of social environment. He is constantly drooling because he leaves his mouth wide open which he needs to wipe it away over and over, and sometimes he does it with his arm, if he does not have his handkerchief, and so forth. Moreover, he is considering his African hairdo, also his out of style fashion which unfortunately attracts people more to ridicule him, instead of modeling after, makes him also very popular around the block, not only for his appearance, but also because of his story with the beautiful blonde on campus that he likes. This friend of mine, I did not mean to paint him in a defamatory way to make fun of, nor to belittle him in any way, not at all, he was a good friend, intelligent, respectful, genuine, and fun to be around with. He happens to love his culture and would love to have somebody from America to share it with, which incidentally happens to be this gorgeous blonde friend of ours that I mentioned earlier.

Anyway, his love, and passion that he has for this young lady was believable, sincere, and genuine, but unfortunately, she did not think she was the one for him, because she too has her own passion and desires in life which among them did not include to marry an African guy, or else to live with him in the continent of Africa. Now, did they end up getting together? No! Mostly because she did not feel the same way about him, and besides she did not have any romantic feeling for him according to what she told us in numerous occasions while we dined together as a group on campus.

You see, the reality is, this friend of mine was living a fantasy that has very little chance of coming true, because his happiness was focused on the wrong thing, he had a wrong understanding of what happiness should be, even though he could have been possible for him to marry the beautiful blonde just like it could have been easily as well for both parties the biggest mistake of their lives to marry each other. Well, I know that many of us have the means, the will, the passion to acquire of something, or somebody may believe that we should go for it at all cost, then when we succeed we may have the time of our lives, the joy that comes with the fact that we accomplish something is the happiness we long for. Perhaps this may be true in many cases because after all, that is the reason we press on in life, because we know once we get there, we will feel great about ourselves, but at the same time we need to remember primarily that we will not find happiness in everything we are pursuing, even though we may have everything we need at our disposal, happiness does not necessarily come in the outcome of what we are pursuing.

Second, to be happy does not mean that everything we desire in life is worth pursuing, because the fact of the matter is, happiness can very well be in the things that we want to have, if we decide not to pursue them, because of the pain, and the grief they may cause us. For example, when it comes to "Sex and Love" we may discover very soon that we had better off to live a life of happiness, if we would distinctively pursue them the way by which they were given to us. In other words, we cannot be happy as we should, when we decide to fashion "Sex and Love" to be our happiness in our ways, for our own gain, and pleasure especially in some avenues of life they are not purposely intended to be.

I know for a fact, and some of you may do as well, that many times a desperate attempt to keep a man so to speak in a romantic relationship is, to allow the sexual act to occur randomly by a desperate woman, which without a doubt can be a superb solution in a short term, but in a long run this mistake will catch up with them both, I am sure with the woman. This random act, played to keep a man in a relationship, is usually the reason by which the relationship cannot survive, because there is a conflict among the two of them, therefore an immediate break up occurs regardless the nature of that relationship at that point.

It frequently happens, that one party in the romantic relationship is more into the relationship about one, than the other. It is because the interest among themselves in the relationship is not mutual, and that is the reason why the one, that supposedly cares more, is always the one that tries to make things happen to maintain the relationship alive at any cost while the other party does not really care for anything; and not only that, sometimes neither one, or the other is not doing anything of some sort to protect what they have. It is only when they realize that their relationship can only survive in an agreement sealed by the authentic mark of an eternal imperative such as marriage, then they would be able to rest peaceably without bringing any form of scheme to so called protect or maintain their relationship. One might ask, what if amid a conflict the one that is more into the relationship solicits sex, and because of it an unwanted pregnancy occurs? Well, as the saying goes "A man will reap what he sows".[6] this is one of many consequences one can face, or must deal with, especially the woman, because she will have to carry the baby and no doubt raise the baby alone. This is the kind of error, among those who are romantically involved, is avoidable possibly when both parties make a good assessment of what it is they want to accomplish in a romantic relationship, without stepping out the boundaries that lay before them.

Now notice the word "LOVE" is a powerful word that is often misunderstood in the arena of romantic relationship, and almost 100% at the time interchanged for sexual entertainment. Thus, to be in love means to be totally sexually attracted or active, else it is not love. Because love is the effect of this wonderful feeling that makes a heart to desire sexual fulfillment to any gender, that is why whenever a person is involved in any form of immorality or sodomy, it is always claimed to have done the act in the name of love as if, it is alright to fornicate, or to sodomite because love is there.[7]

Love has become the common denominator for everybody's infraction in human relationship when falling in diverse temptations in doing what's not supposed to be doing, once being caught love is the automatic default answer. For example, a thirteen-year-old girl is kissing with a fifteen-year-old boy in the back of the school every time school lets out, if you were to ask them why they are doing that, they would tell because they love each other "Love". Why is love always the quick answer even when someone does wrong in a relationship, or not in a relationship at all?

By the way, to be in the safe side, "Love" is being used here in the context of the world's view of love and understanding, since there are no boundaries as to which the world extends its arrogance makes it almost impossible to distinguish true and pure love among human race relationship, because of all the layers of garbage that are being produced for the sake of happiness. For this cause, the world is in rage, and furious, in protecting its work by beguiling more and more the humans into becoming less moral through the channel of sexual impurity with all kinds of pervasive activities just in a brink of time which will carry consequences for all eternity.

Therefore, it is imperative to identify the tricks of this world to make sure that, as human beings, we avoid them at all costs, not to buy into them, but in the effort to go back to the foundation to draw from the spring of stainless love and natural as it was once given to us. Sexual activities should not be something that we are fearful about, knowing the uncertainty after we've done it whether we are going to be well emotionally, or not and physically, or perhaps to live with guilt knowing fully that we have violated the fundamental principles of such relationship, because we've been influenced by the world's directives to make believe that everything is alright for our enjoyment because we practice the so called safe sex.

Needless to say, if there was such a thing called safe sex in the world out there, it would not be offered to us freely, it would without a doubt be offered to us with a great price tag which would almost be impossible for us to get our hands on it.

Unfortunately, there is such a thing called safe sex which the world does not have because safe sex simply is not a product of the world. The world can only offer something which was in its purest form tamed by the world and used by it to promote its agenda because safe sex can only be practiced within the bond of marriage which protects one man for one woman, and one woman for one man, or perhaps the other alternative would be to abstain from any sexual activities before marriage period. That's what safe sex is all about!

Safe sex is about knowing the difference between what is lawful and unlawful, not only that, safe sex is not something that you get, it is something that is given to you or received, so unless you've been given a partner for life, by that I mean a heterosexual relationship, a relationship between one man and one woman as it was instituted, not by whatever else the world wants it to be, you cannot practice safe sex, because safe is not a matter of convenience that is to say, make sure you use condoms, or other forms of preservative to protect you from STD, or perhaps to avoid pregnancy. These provisions are only an effort to camouflage your presence into the battle field of sexual activities, but the fact remains that you've been involved, and because of your involvement in such a way outside the bond of marriage, you are positioned yourself against the fundamental law of sexual engagement, therefore you are guilty.

The last thing you want to have on your back is to carry with you the burden of guilt for the rest of your life for something that you cannot undo. It is going to be forever before you regardless of your regret. Sex and love are products of the same emotional seed, yet different from one another in essence, and in practice, because one can be, sadly to say, sexually active with someone not necessarily be in love with that someone vice a versa in relationship. Perhaps you are wondering why two elements of the same kind can be totally different from each other?

Number one reason can be because love is a process, it takes time to build, it works through a series of choices, and it establishes trust and protects each other's interests in cultivating a long-term relationship by keeping promises with truth and character. Number two reason, love is not cunning, it seeks always the welfare of the other first without selfish motive, it exercises mutual respect and looking out for each other in good and tough times. Number three reason, love is always demonstrated through positive actions and virtuous deeds always because love is by nature sacrificial **I Cor. 13.**[8]

But when it comes to sex, it always works through a physical attraction, just to say, one is pleased based on what meets the eyes, in other words, and if you like them you want them. Many a time a man likes a woman vice a versa because of the physical feature that attracts the opposite sex toward the other which in turn creates a sexual feeling to be had even just for a moment. When a man likes a woman vice a versa because of his or her lips, it is not love, it is sexual attraction. When a woman likes a man because of his physic, it is not love, it is sexual attraction because the reaction toward the young man's physic is only based on the desire to deliciously savor that young man just in the nick of time regardless of whom he is, or any other factors of his life.

Perhaps you've seen and heard women's reaction when they see a well- dressed man passing by, such reaction is none other than sexual. It is sexual because the intent is to provoke this man character into believing that he is powerful, and that he can have whatever his heart desires even to know any woman in a sexual manner right away, because the suit gives him that power. When a man also meets a very attractive woman with an apparel of a cleavage reveals more than it should the area of her chest, the man's reaction toward that is not love, but rather sexual because in his heart he breaks God's law in the way he looks at the woman (**Matt. 5:28**).

The bottom line is this, it is very easy to fall into the category of sexual attraction many times more than to be involved romantically cultivated with somebody, that is why a lot of people get confused when things like that happen to them because they believe when they experience a kind of feeling toward someone, it must be telling them something, after all they have never felt that way before for someone, and because their heart is beating faster than usual, it must be the one, therefore, they believe that they are in love. Some people even call it "Love at first sight" because even though they may have been sexually active in the past with someone, their heart has never been beaten so hard for anyone like that in their lifetime, so it could be a sign.

Yes! It is a sign, it is rather a sign of disappointment awaiting down the road to happen because when it comes to love as it relates to two people of the opposite sexes to share their lives together, the heart is always going to lead to desires, wants, feelings, regrets, which brings conflicts, which brings disagreement which also brings fight, and fight which ultimately brings separation. And when that happens in a romantic relationship that was not sit on the principles of pure love, with multiple occasions of sexual activities, the guilt factor will kick in, and begin to make life miserable because of all the transactions that have been going on consequently, in trying to fulfill your heart's desires.

You've often time heard people say: "Follow your heart" in other words, what they are saying is this, do anything you want according to your heart's desires. Honestly, this is a foolish way to live your life, if each time you've come to this one juncture of your life, to make a crucial decision and you leave it at the mercies of your heart's desires, can you imagine the impact? Perhaps you've never thought of it that way, but for the most part you've made decisions like that which caused you a great deal of pain, where you don't know how you're going to get rid of it. Again, a decision that is vital such as to be in love with somebody for the rest of your life, shouldn't be made as your heart leads, it should be made on the principles by which two people can come together to abide on the agreement they'll live for, in a relationship that allows them to do so without regrets, or guilt even after sex because they are soundly hinged on the premise of the law of matrimony, the basis by which they will be one **Gen. 24.**[9]

With that in mind, there is an order all human being should follow to walk in agreement with the law of sexual engagement. The order is that everyone of us needs to start seeing people in quest for love first, and then as the relationship grows stronger, in marriage, sex will be a benefit among many for being in love with each other, not the other way around. It will be too much of a hassle to try to find love after being sexually involved with someone, it does not work that way. Love is the leader not sex, if you love someone you will have sex with (in compliance with the fundamental principle of course), but if you have sex with someone you will not love him just for that, vice a versa.

Perhaps you may love only to have sexual relationship with that preferred someone in the context of fulfilling your sexual desires, but not emotionally connected to be with that person as a life partner. You know, everything we've talked about in this segment is of a vital importance for every human being on the planet earth, because this issue is essential to develop character in the life of everyone, not only that, but it is also essential to keep man and woman from falling into the lie of sexual libertine in destroying their lives to be rather brought together in the proper context of such relation as it was intended to be from the beginning.

Once again, my utmost sincere appeal as an author, as a parent, or as a friend, is on the parents to be more than ever involved in building character, solid teaching of discernment from right and wrong in the life of their children as they grow older continuously, so that they in turn would have something to live with, and to pass on to their children in the hope of a bright and safe tomorrow.

Remember "Love and sex" can be great assets and tools in human relationship when they apply in the proper context of every day's relationship between one man and one woman to enjoy, to preserve the human race by means of reproduction, and to be presented as a banner of righteousness, so that the little ones can model from, but unfortunately if it reverse where we have "Sex and love" it can be a liability among the human race for its destruction, and also the abolishment of character, and moral conduct, which can be also a banner of unrighteousness as a model to follow after, where there will be no hope for a bright and safe tomorrow. That's why both parents and lovers of justice need to stand united in fighting together against liberal ideology, or anything else that can harm our children and their future, and their children's future by being vigilant and firm to our conviction, in returning to the old fashion way of bringing boys and girls to the real teaching of "Sex education" as we put up a fence of protection around them to know from right and wrong about "Love and Sex". And to finally throw out of the windows of the world, the relativism teaching of whatever they want "Love and Sex" to be for their own good, and for the betterment of a society.

For this cause, let us take a stand against alcoholism, drinking, drugs and any other substances, or activities that can be detrimental for our young people and ourselves if we want to be good examples to them. Also let us encourage our young people to be good agents out there, in protecting themselves and others, in upholding the truth, to be good citizens in making effort to abide and respect principles that are set before them, we as parents also would make sure they are supervised throughout their life as they are becoming adult, also to take on responsibilities as well for their own children. Parents make no mistakes, if we fail our children we fail to do our job, and we will certainly fail as a nation, a society, and most definitely as a human race, we will be no different from the animal beings.

"To every thing there is a season and a time
To every purpose under the heaven:
A time to be born and a time to die;
A time to plant, and a time to pluck up that
Which is planted;
A time to kill, and a time to heal;
A time to break down, and a time to build up;
A time to weep, and a time to laugh; a time
to mourn, and a time to dance;
a time to cast away stones and a time to gather
stones together; a time to embrace, and a time to
refrain from embracing;
a time to get, and a time to lose, a time to keep
and a time to cast away;
a time to rend, and a time to sew; a time to keep
silence, and a time to speak;
a time to love, and a time to hate; a time
of war, and a time of peace" **Eccl. 3:1-8.**[1]

Giving the scope of our society in sexual performances daily, I think it is evident that everyone can be sexually involved one way, or another. Perhaps we don't need to worry too much in knowing whether, or not if they can be sexually involved, for they are involved already, but instead we need to market a solution to help putting into right perspective the real reason to be involved sexually, which in turn will give them a sense of worth, to be able to understand the why, the when, and the who. Needless to say, young and old alike are more deliberately involved sexually than ever before with the help of internet pornography, magazines, books, and TV shows makes it available to them 24 hrs a day. Today more and more young people are rigorously exercising to be in decent shape, some would take substances that would stimulate, or enhance their sex drive to perform better and longer sexually. Others like older folks would go through sex therapy sessions regularly, or even would engage on a sex drug stimulant such as Viagra, Cialis, and others in order even at an older age to be able to still perform well, and longer sexually. [2]

Therefore, sex has become a commodity at the reach of everybody's convenience, even to the point where everybody is talking about it everywhere, at the bus station, on the train, the airplane, at work, at the dinner table, on the football field without reservation because sex is right now the hottest topic in the market, also everybody's favorite. We have allowed ourselves to unashamedly disclose information about our sex life to the public either for money mostly, or for fame through magazines, and television shows such as "Jerry Springer, Maurey show, Tara show, divorce court" to name a few whereas this information should have kept private for the most part, have become subject of ridicule over the air waves, and at the same time encouraged others to do the same for the sake of entertainment and the freedom of free speech.

From the second part of the 20th century to thus far in the 21st century, things have gotten extremely bad, when it comes to morality, especially in the sexual conduct area. It seems as if there are no boundaries as to what people can do in this avenue. They plan, they organize, they destroy, they sacrifice lives, so that they can simply even for one-time deal satisfy their lustful desires, by engaging themselves in many kinds of sexual activities which have without a doubt, painful consequences because of their action upon themselves, and their family as well. No wonder people everywhere are so sexually minded, they are like animal beings led to be slaughtered in a hand full, they are acting as if they do not have the sense of right and wrong when it comes to this matter even at the expense of their life, they don't care because their mind has been saturated for so long with the wrong kind of information that can only have one to wonder the reality of everyone is sexually involved.

Unfortunately, the condition by which everyone today, supposedly to be sexually involved, is not the ideal one in general, for the fact that, it produces more damages than it should, and at the same time undermines the very foundation upon which humanity should stand morally that sets him apart from the animal beings in a society where both cohabit. If we do not draw the line as human beings that ethically changes the modality of our lives for the better, we will in fact become like animals, live like them, act like they do, behave like they do, ultimately it would seem to be true that we are descendants of monkey, we're just simply evolved, what a tragedy!

We have been given the opportunity to be birthed into this world with tremendous potentials to be supreme beings over the animals, and to rule over them, not to become like them, or else to be worse than they. The animals are what they are because they do not have the faculty to make good choices, good judgments, and to make difference between right and wrong, therefore they cannot reason for themselves, they need us to do that for them, they cannot instruct themselves to behave fairly, they need us to help them with that, they cannot care for themselves when they get hurt, they need us to do that for them, and so many other things in the animals lives that they need they cannot do for themselves, we do for them. Likewise, we are indeed capable to behave the same way they do behave, but the only thing that keeps us apart from them, and by the way, it makes an enormous difference, is the fact that we know as human beings what is right and what is wrong, other than that, it would not have a distinction between human beings and animal beings.

Yes! Everyone can be sexually involved at any time, but it does not give a license to us to be involved in such a way any time, everywhere, anyhow, with anyone we want to, like the animal beings would do. We as human beings we have rules to consider when it comes to sexual activities, if we disregard the rules, we're acting as if we do not possess the faculty to know right from wrong. We are creatures of knowledge, and we always need to make decisions based on the knowledge that was set before us in everything, so that we can operate in the realm of humans, if ever we want to be considered as such. There has not been any other creature upon, above, or beneath the earth that rules were given to, except only human beings because we are the only creatures that can operate with them and cannot without them. Be as it may, we must abide by the rules set before us as well as other rules when it comes to sexual conduct to set us apart from the animal beings.

There is a season in fact for everything in life and a purpose for the privileges that have been given to us even the privilege of being sexually involved with someone else. Notice, sexual activities normally have little to do with your desires, in fact to be in the safe side your desires will always lead you astray, because your desires will come and go, and most of all, they are not founded on any sure foundation where you should feel secure. There is the insecurity of catching up this venereal disease, the insecurity of being trapped on an unwanted pregnancy, or a relationship with a stranger, the insecurity of being exposed your involvement with a specific person to the public, and many other types of insecurity in this arena. Your life in relationship with sexual activities should be viewed like a plant that is being planted waiting for the right season to bear its fruits.

For example, a mango tree when its seed is being put in the ground, this seed must endure the process from the moment it touches the ground to where it would start to germinate in the formation of its fruit bearing. Then when the mangos are ripe, people can begin to enjoy the succulent taste of the mango's seed that has been planted in the ground for lengthy period in the past five, or six years approximately.[3] So you see, the mango would not have been able to produce succulent mangos with savoring taste, had it not been left in the ground to go through the process from being a seed to become a grown mature mango tree. The same it is for every human being to understand that each life on this planet earth has a purpose, and this purpose can only be accomplished once that life is given the opportunity to go through the process from its prime to the fullest of its maturity to be considered worthwhile, otherwise it would be a wasted life even when it appears to be a mature life, it will accomplish nothing. That is why sexual involvement should be evidence of going through the process of becoming mature to where fruit bearing is possible in its proper context at the right moment of one's life.

When the seed was in the ground, it was not up to the sower to decide when the seed should begin to sprout, nor was it his decision to speed up the process in order to harvest mangos sooner than expected, but instead he needed to wait for as long as the process should take to be able to succeed until the harvest come because the success of this seed to become a mango tree and his success as a sower depends on his willingness to wait to the end. So likewise, it is imperative for us as human beings to understand that we cannot or should not in any form trying to speed up the process of our lives to be sexually involved outside the proper context of such involvement, just because we decide to fulfill our sexual desires. For every time we decide to break the process to where we have not come to full maturity at the right place and at the right time to accomplish our purpose in this area of our lives, we fail and not only that, we also are in contradiction with ourselves as to where we are supposed to be in the process.

Therefore, we violate the rules, our lives begin to ruin, and we are bound to be tossed aside because we are unfortunately worth nothing. That is exactly what would happen to the seed if the sower of the seed decided to speed up the process to make the seed to produce fruits earlier than its time expected. It would be impossible to make that to happen despite of his effort to want the process to continue, he would ruin it, and finally he would have to toss it away, oh! What a waste! Remember rules are present in our lives for protection, they allow us to operate safely without looking over our shoulders to see if we are being watched, they give us the freedom to walk with confidence with humbleness of heart, and to speak boldly the truth without hesitation.

Often time we heard that rules are meant to be broken when in fact, what it means is, broken rules are equal broken lives. Every time a person is in trouble, it is always because the result of him breaking the law, or some rules established. No one ever gets punished for doing something right, but instead punishment comes because of wrongdoing always. Therefore, we need to teach our children well from infantile to grown up adulthood that dreadful things always happen when you disobey. We certainly do not want to inflict more pain and suffering upon our lives deliberately, but unfortunately that is what we are doing every time we put ourselves in violation with the law, we are acting as if we are saying, here we are we want to get hurt.

Perhaps you are probably saying what is the purpose of one waiting for a long time to be sexually involved when in fact he is old enough and has the means necessary to do what he wants to do? This question opens the door to the reality that is out there that everybody thinks he/she has the right to satisfy his/her sexual desires anytime the opportunity comes. Now the question is where does that right come from? I do believe this right is as an excuse to proceed to do what it is we want to do; we usually claim that we have the right of this, or that when in fact what we have is an opportunity to serve in upholding the laws, or the rules that were established before we came on the scene. We disregard the rules because we think that we are not kids anymore, or even if we were still, we believe that we are free to make our own decisions, to make our own choices regardless the rules.

For example, you know as well as I do, if you work for an employer, you are expected to be at the workplace at the time appointed, also you are expected to remain there until your time is up because if you fail to do so, you will be asked to leave indefinitely. I am certain when this employer lays out the ground rule before you, you will do nothing less except to comply with the regulations so that you can have a place to work and bring home with you a paycheck, so that you can take care of yourself and your family. It won't be matter to you whether you like the rules, or not, you will do all you can to uphold the rules regardless of your preference because you know once you abide by the rules, it not only protects your job, but it also secures your paycheck, and therefore, you will be well taken care of. Likewise, if you could understand it from a perspective of an employer and employee relationship, you should have no problem to agree to uphold the rules of sexual engagement no matter your desires may be, because by being in the same page with the rules, your life will be well protected, your future will be secured, and you will accomplish your purpose in life until the day you will be asked to departure this earth.

Your purpose in this life is to keep yourself pure in abstaining from any inappropriate sexual conduct, or immorality before, during, and after marriage relationship, because when sexual relation was given to us only with the rules as to how we should benefit from it, and act on it. I will venture to say that the only people who should freely talk about sexual relation are supposed to be the married couples because they are the ones that fit the criteria by which two people can be sexually involved, they are the ones who should also know about it.

For this cause, here are the rules we should know to be compliant with sexual involvement.

1. We are created to remain virgin until we cleave to another person in marriage. That is one man and one-woman vice and versa (**Gen. 2: 21-22**).
2. We are not created to be with multiple partners sexually (**Gen. 2:24**).
3. We are only created to be with one man and one woman at a time (**Gen. 2: 25**).
4. Marriage relationship between one man and one woman is the only platform for sexual involvement (**Gen. 2: 24-25**).

5. Life is only created to be joined with one man and one woman not to be shared with anybody else we desire (**Gen. 2:22**).

6. Once we find that special someone for our lives, that is one man or one woman, there should be no sexual act apart from the person we 're married to (**Gen. 24:67; I Thess. 4: 1-5; Prov. 5: 15-19**).

7. Once we're married, we are married for life until death do us part (**Gen. 2:24; Matt. 19: 5-6**).

8. Marriage is also the only platform given by God to bring children into this world (**Gen. 1: 27-28**).

9. Marriage is the only place created for a man and a woman to become one, not one man with another man, or one woman with another woman (**Gen. 2: 23-25; Matt. 19: 5-6**).

10. Sexual relation can only be protected in a marriage relationship and can also be proven that we as human beings are not monkey's descendants (**Gen. 1: 26-27; Gen. 2: 21-23**).[4]

At this time, you've come to realization that apart from a marriage relationship, no one should get involved sexually according to the right standard to uphold, so that we can be protected and enjoyed the normalcy of a great relationship between a man and a woman. Apparently for some of us when we were growing up, we did have parents, or guardians throughout the ages of our formation to guide us into the right paths, and we were obedient to them and adhered to their principles which as a result of our obedience we have been spared from a lot of troubles, pain, suffering, difficulties of this life, where at this moment we are truly grateful for their commitment, hard work, and sacrifices they made to bring us up in the admonition and right path of this life. For without their help and their consistency to keep us on the right track as parents, we probably would not be here today.

For those of us who were privileged to have parents, who cared enough for their children, even through discipline with strong conviction to shield us from being involved in some of the libertine sexual activities out there, are indeed living proofs of what clear and right teaching of sexual relation can impact the lives of children whose parents are not afraid to take a stand to bring them up in the right way. Unfortunately for those of us whose parents were cowardly reluctant to engage in the upbringing of their children while letting them to be brought up at the mercies of some TV program, friends, or perhaps nannies, or day care centers might have been the causes for which their children did not turn out to be ok a bit later in life. They became rebellious toward authorities, they did not stay in school, they also involved in all types of sexual pervasions earlier in life, they became immoral, and because of their upbringing they want to rationalize everything they do wrong and blame it on somebody else. Therefore, they become selfish, they have an intolerable attitude, ultimately, they have no goals in life, and basically no hope for a better future.

Perhaps if you are a parent, you are probably saying this would never happen to my children. Well, let me ask you this. Are you supervising them in their daily activities? Are you letting them know that you will monitor all their activities anywhere and everywhere regardless whom they are with? Basically, they are going to be chaperoned whenever they are out with mix group, do you tell them that? Your life, your children's life is serious business to undertake, it needs close supervision and accountability, just like you need, or everybody needs to take care of his body hygienically every day to keep it from being sick and decayed, so the same does your body and everybody's else body for that matter need to be kept clean sexually and from any types of sexual pervasion and immorality. It is not a way to force anybody's preference, or opinion on someone else's life, but it is in effect an effort for everybody to stay safe, clean, pure from destroying oneself in this area of life which was given to us at the same time for our enjoyment once practiced in the proper context.

Often time as parents, we begin to do it right with our children in the first chapter of their lives, we teach them the proper way to brush their teeth, the proper way to address people, the proper way to sit at the table to eat a meal, the proper way to exercise to stay in good shape physically, the proper way to behave socially, and to do all kinds of things properly, so that they can involve and progress in this life, but when it comes to the second chapter of their lives, we tend to back down, we kind of letting them take care of things on their own, especially at the prime of their adulthood life. We believe that they are old enough to make decisions for themselves as to however they want to manage their life, it seems as if they are free to choose to destroy themselves because they are grown ups, it is not up to us parents anymore because they supposed to make up for all the years they had to obey and listen to us.

Therefore, when they go out to party, it is ok for them to be drinking, it is ok for them to be fornicating all they want to whomever they want, and they come here and brag about it as if everything is alright, why? Because you say it is ok! It is not ok whether they begin to be sexually active, or not at the age of their adulthood, or even sooner. The point being here is, the fact that they should have a foundation by which they can tell the difference between what is lawful and unlawful (speaking in a traditional way here) because all they should have in mind is to be looking forward for this awesome and wonderful day when legally and fundamentally they would present themselves as a clean vessel to whoever they would marry on that day with the greatest smile on their faces where as you would stand tall in that wedding ceremony with nothing in your heart, that you have done your job in preserving that which you have received from the day of their births, in giving it freely to the one who has the right to take it with grace and humbleness of heart.

Up to that point you would know that your child has been protected for that hand you are giving in marriage for the rest of their lives, not only that, but you would have a chance to witness the fruit of your hard works, the legacy of a well- founded tradition to carry on to the next generation. That's what it's all about to be proud parents, even in a society where it seems there is no way to do the right thing.

For everything there is a season, if you know the alternative when in fact no one seems to care to bring up the children in the right way, in adopting the sentiment of laissez faire, you are going to work even harder, so that you can get to that season and it will be worth it. Your children will be happier, and they too will follow your footsteps and ultimately, it will come back to the same principle "... whatsoever a man soeth that shall he also reap" **Gal. 6:7.**[5] and finally every family will prevail to remain as a unit. There will be no broken marriages, no broken home, there will be no children outside of marriage, also any children being born out of wedlock, and assuredly there will be no step family, or divorce.

These assumptions are being made for the fact we are dealing with human relationship, which somehow was not handled properly, because of that, it brought separation. Be as it may, if the relationship of those who went through divorce to become step parents has been properly channeled through the fundamental principles of human relationship such as marriage, they would not have to rethink and try at it the second time around, the first time would have been alright. It is not by accident that couples struggle so much in their marriages, it is either there has been sexual relation before marriage among themselves, or other partners, also because there is continual sexual relation taken place with another partner while being married. Make no mistakes; there will be problems when these activities are constantly present in a marriage. Whenever there is something foreign to the marriage relationship, it will surface through hardship, difficulties, fights, and even divorce. Just like it is in a garden planted with good seeds in the soil, once there come weeds growing up at the same time with the good seeds, automatically these weeds are going to kill the good seeds if they are not taken care of.

In all sincerity, human relationship is no different from the good seeds and the weeds because each person has been created to live with one partner only regardless of his opinion, it would not be matter for the fact that marriage relationship is a lifetime commitment, it is until death due you part, it was not meant to be broken, it was made with the same idea of the good seeds in the ground, once being planted it was meant to be planted, not to be planted in one field and later on to be plucked up and planted again in another field. No! It must endure the process to get to the level of maturity, so that it can bring forth fruits, which in turn can reproduce other seeds the same kind which can be planted in another field and so forth. That is the reason why, it is vitally important that we as human beings understand the reality of our lives regarding properly execute the fundamental principles by which we all were created, so that we can all avoid at all cost the suffering, the pain, and the hardship of life once we violate, or ignore the fundamental principles.

You all know as well as I do that our success depends on the choices that we make, and so does our failure. Our choices should be choices that align themselves with the fundamental principles of life, not should they be paralleled to them, or against them. Believe it or not, once our choices are against the principles of life, we begin to create problems not only for ourselves, but also for others, and perhaps for the next generation to come.

Life itself was not given to us to be complicated as we are living it, it begins with the first family of the humans who decided to violate the fundamental principles set before them once, in disobeying the standard which they should have followed, consequently brought all of us to a world of desolation, despair, pain, suffering, sickness, and death. Think about it! For so long we have been suffered all kind of difficulties throughout our lives from generations prior to ours and many generations to come unfortunately.

Now it is time that we should make decisions individually and collectively to pledge to adhere by the principles of life which have been over our heads for so long. As an individual we should recognize our limitations and exercise abstinence to uphold the principles, and to protect ourselves from the consequences of breaking them. As collectively, we need to resolve to refrain from any activity that stands in violation of the principles established, and not only that, we need to campaign in promoting good behavior, good choices, and banish all kinds of inappropriate activities that we have been doing that brought us to where we are now. Because of all that, we will be free to make good choices anytime regardless the matter, and all together we should stand in denouncing all immorality among ourselves, and purposely take charge to abolish the works of suspected immoral behavior anywhere they are. With that in mind, it is time to pluck up these bad seeds that have been with us for so long, and to plant good ones so that we can live life in a different brand-new way where life in abundance and happiness will be flourishing.

I DON'T LOVE YOU I AM IN IT JUST FOR SEX

Two generations ago precisely the generations of my grandfathers and grandmothers, (unfortunately I did not have a chance to know both of my grandmothers because they died when both my parents were still kids) perhaps the generations before them as well had a custom by which men and women would engage romantically. Their custom was, when a man was old enough to be married, when he had an interest on a particular woman in the neighborhood, what he would do first, if he was a singer, a guitar player, or a banjo player per se, he would go by night to where the young lady of interest is sleeping at her house, him and a few other guys would sing and play music in a romantic way expressing his love manifesto in the songs to that young lady throughout all night until dawn so no one else in the neighborhood would suspect who he was. This gentleman and his bodies would continue to come at night by this young lady's house to sing his heart out in asking for her love.[1]

Sometimes, this serenade would go on for days, and months in and out. Usually if the young man is not a singer, or a banjo player, or a guitar player, he would pay a group of men called "The Troubadours" to come to sing and play romantic songs in the honor of that young lady. Imagine many nights my grandfather would tell me that the young man would go without sleep and the money that he would spend to win the young lady's heart. The idea through of this was, when the young man finally would win the young lady's heart, she would show herself, by the window of the house where she stays, to the young man with two gifts in her hands. The gifts are a handkerchief, and a small bottle of cologne which she would hand to the young man indicating that she accepts his love. Some people would speculate over the years that the handkerchief was to be a symbol of her virginity, and the cologne was the essence of her faithfulness to him. It has been said, that many later have found out that the ladies were not indeed virgin and they did not remain faithful for the most part in the relationship before, or after they got married.[2]

Furthermore, when words got out that the men were being deceived, being played for fools, they went on to sing and play songs for the ladies only to get to know them sexually first with the promise that they would eventually marry them. And so, this would go on for years until the ladies said they had enough of it, they would not sleep with the guys, if only and only they would marry them first to make them their wives, then they would enjoy sexual relationship other than that they are not going to play the guys' games. So, my grandfather would tell me that the game between the sexes was playing for a while when at last the ladies realized they were still in their forty's, they we're still not getting married because the guys did not want to show any interest in them. That is how it all began when men and women started to be together, living in the same house not necessarily married to each other, and even having children where many men would say they did not father their kids and so forth.

In those days even though the kids might have been this man's kids, there was no way to prove it, no technology in place at that time to initiate a paternity test, so they all got away with the lie even knowing deep in their heart that they were indeed the father of those kids they were having. Later on because of so many kids all over the place in the country and more specifically in the cities whose fathers could not be identified, a law had to be passed and kept by many other administrations following, that if a man fathers a child and refuses to accept the child as his own, if there is a slightly sign of resemblance between the child and the supposed father, if he continue to refuse to take care of the child, he will be put in jail for the rest of his life and be charged with child abandonment. Since this law has been passed, my grandfather told me that all the traditions regarding men and women romantic relationship have been banished, and people started to live differently where parents such as those of my grandparents would not have a legacy to maintain because there was not one.[3] As a matter fact, my father's father did not marry his mother; he refused to accept him (my father) as his child. Therefore, my father did not bear his name, but instead his mother's name.

To recognize in fact when somebody accepted to father a child was when the child carried the man's last name. In my case, had my father's father given him his last name, my last name would have been Charles instead Fenelon because Charles was supposed to be his last name. And I was fortunate enough to hear this from my grandfather some years before he passed on, he wanted me to have an idea of the things he had experienced from his days in comparison to the way things had become in our days. He wanted me to be careful when I become older in the time to seek for a bride that I would not be influenced by the culture to destroy my life, my future just before it begins. He was wise enough to notice that today's culture is not in quest for love, to settle down to have a normal ordinary family, but he saw that most couples in a relationship are not in it for love, but they are in the relationship just for sex. That is why my grandfather would say, they do not want to accept the idea of marriage relationship because why bother marrying if they can have sex without marriage whether they fall in love or not. It does not need a rocket science to notice the message that is being propagated in the fundamental behavior of our today's culture regarding romantic relationship, particularly between a man and a woman, and the message is none other than "I don't love you, I am in it just for sex".[4]

Yes, indeed, in today's culture it is not a foreign idea among supposed lovers, but rather common that they are enjoying each other for the time being before they would get in a committed relationship, meaning marriage. Sometimes the excitement that somewhat they would make it to the next level is banished unfortunately at the first stage of their relationship, because the excitement was only an excitement to want to be with each other, but it was not pursued with a purpose in mind to a concrete agenda which determines where they want to be in the years to come.

Furthermore, if they have one, they do not know how to cultivate it to get to that point, because they totally neglect the path that leads them to where they want to be. Their mindset regarding romantic relationship is not in favor of upholding the truth to abstain from any kinds of impurity during the time of their romantic involvement. The normal that is out there in any romantic relationship right now is to make sure you do whatever you can to keep him/her happy for as long as he/she is happy, because there is a chance that the relationship can make it to the next level. Therefore, marriage is no longer a platform for sexual involvement, and reproduction, and lifetime commitment, but instead it becomes a social formality at the convenience of whoever desires to have it whether good, or bad. That is the reason why young people at the earliest of age seek to conform with the culture's mandate concerning romantic relationship, because they don't have to commit in such relationship, for it is acceptable among them to uncover that which was forbidden to uncover, so that they can be in perfect tune with the culture.

Besides, they would not hesitate to engage sexually because they do have at their disposal materials such as: pornographic magazines, books, videos, condoms, birth control pills, and lubricants to both stimulate their sexual appetite, and ultimately to have a pleasurable moment. These kinds of activities are happening right now every day in our culture, where old and mostly our young people are fully engaged with their eyes closed in relying with the teaching they are receiving from schools, kid's clubs, and others in the name of sex education that it is perfectly normal to enjoy their life in such a way, for it is for their own good. It is rather precarious to rationalize when it comes to sexual activities. Remember I mentioned before that sexual relation was the door by which you entered this world; it can also be the door by which you get out this world depending on how you view yourself in the arena of life. Engaging sexually before marriage is not automatically the end of one's life, but it is in fact a detour in the wrong way in one's life, if it is not corrected.

It is like driving down the road with your eyes closed, or perhaps a ship lost at sea.

These illustrations show the predicaments one can find himself in, if driving with eyes close in the road, and the uncertainty to make it to the shore is very present, because one must understand that eyes are very important for driving, and a maritime map is vitally important to voyage at sea. The same, sexual involvement is icing on the cake in a marriage. Keep in mind, in this life's journey we are all in together, we all have been given the ability to discern from right and wrong, also to make choices according to our discernment so that we can live our lives as results of those choices to make the best of ourselves in everything even when we fail, we can still manage to get back up to go on with the journey to be successful no matter how powerful the challenges may be. There are truly numerous aids out there that supposedly help in leaning toward excellence when pursuing a romantic relationship, where unfortunately in following their advice we end up falling deeper in the pit of ignorance and guilt.

Such aids are for examples ABC's television series "The bachelor, or the bachelorette" NBC's "For love, or for money", and other television series that somehow deal with romantic relationship. Unfortunately, these series of television shows define to the public what they want you to believe love is, in offering their help via entertainment, where the products they are selling are seemingly authentic at heart, but purely counterfeit. The system upon which they operate gives a sense of security that somehow captivates the attention of many groups of viewers, and perhaps the most fragile ones, and especially those who have been on the romantic road before but failed and wished to bounce back once again this time only with a different approach. That is why, those television shows bring solace to the hopeless at love, or to many who somehow have been through a difficult road not necessarily being abused, or mistreated at all, it just simply they did not know how to be in a romantic relationship, but because they have been selfish and ignorant at best in involving with interpersonal relationship. Because of such dilemma they believe that they may be unlovable, or they do not have luck at love, so when television shows like that come on the air, they sort of ignited by them, to give another shot at love even though in the back of their head they are making a fool of themselves, but because of what they are being drawn to, the images they have seen through the screen of their television set, they just accept it all as true romance and love with such eager to be part of the ambiance, and they at the same time fail to critically analyze the product, they buy into it, they want it and they go for it.[5]

Naturally, if you are looking at the development of these television shows you might think in a contemporary sense that they are harmless to the detriment of a society because first, they reflect the character of its society at the best. Second, they kind of like helping the society to stay on track of who they are as people in revealing their sexuality not to hide it, but to tolerate diversity from a sexual point of view no matter what they do, it ought not to bother anybody because it is in fact a way of life. But on the other side, if you look at it from a conservative point of view you will realize it is in fact the reflection of the society at its best, and yes, it is helping the society to stay on track to counter the truth about society not by the way it is revealing in the society, but the way it should have been handled within the society as principle. It is of no surprise, when dealing with critical subject such as love in the society that the source for standard is always the passive option, that includes a vague reasoning of acceptable truths as oppose to dogmatic solution that says, this is right, or this is wrong.

With that in mind, it makes it so much easier for people who've been hurt emotionally, after being in a romantic relationship chaos, to look for another romantic relationship to recover with the intention to have a better relationship than the previous one, to choose the help of ABC's television shows, and NBC's, but not realizing that they are going to end up in the same dilemma they found themselves before, just because they simply changed the characters in the play while they are still operating on the same ideology that brought them ill.

For this reason, it is important that society finds another alternative, in other words, to stop absorbing any sort of teaching that compromises the truth, to avoid emotional pain and hurt by embracing a dogmatic alternative by which you can depend on for safe romantic relationship, both physically and emotionally. Nobody is above the law, or immune to emotional hurt, it can be prevented when follow this dogmatic principle as a road map for romantic relationship success. It is emphatically a guaranteed success for those of us who choose to accept the alternative road for a romantic relationship from a dogmatic point of view, or the traditional way over those who refuse this pathway, they can always expect failure, and damaging outcome, because there is not a sure foundation upon which their relationship is built on, or a road map, it is instead let's figure it out kind of thing as you go, which demonstrates a lack of understanding of how it is both parties should relate to each other romantically, or perhaps it is clearly evident among themselves that they do not want to project a fair conclusion, but rather they are just in the relationship just to enjoy each other's company sexually.

Oh, friend what a pity! The idea of two people of the opposite sexes to be together in the marriage relationship shouldn't be a price tag like you would normally have to buy an outfit in an apparel store, so that you would compare it with other friends of their relationship to see who's got the best love bargain. It is not necessarily important to compare one romantic relationship with another; the simple reason is for the fact that every relationship is unique to itself, or every person in any relationship is also different from one person to another. That's what makes the relationship worth having, because each person brings a personal flavor to that relationship, so that he/ she can explore the dynamic of every individual's uniqueness in such level.

Later, when things begin to turn sour in the relationship,

each one of them can draw back at the time of the beginning of their relationship substances that made them unique as a couple and different from other couples to lean on these substances that were once ideal to mend the relationship once again no matter the situation may be as they are going through it.

That is what makes love worth seeking because it really puts in perspective the reality of what it is two people of opposite sexes should have to be together, and not only that, it begins to reveal with clarity the purpose for which you were created, so that you can begin to live life with no fear of breaking any laws, specifically the law of sexual involvement, and at the same time manifest the benefits for choosing to live a life of purity, truth, character, equity, and guilt free as a model for others to follow.

There may be this contagious sentiment of our day that it is a must that couple should be sexually involved before marriage, because that is an obvious choice to make and perhaps that is the reason such tendency is prevalent in our society, but it is also important to know even though sexual involvement may be an obvious choice to make among the sexes before marriage, that there are those who separate themselves to not being influenced by this society's trend to believe that it is humanly impossible to abstain from sexual act before marriage. There is no doubt that the challenge is going to be greater among those who are willing to stay away from sexual impurity than among those who are giving in to it, but it would be worth to do so because the benefits of accepting the challenge would also be much, much greater, there shall be no regret for those who wait. In fact, you will be better off because you were not in violation with the law of sexual involvement, you wouldn't have to worry about anything at this point as far as guilt, remorse, and so forth, you would be completely satisfied to be able to stand blameless in pursuing happiness, peace, and prosperity.

Really, there is no guaranty in life since you've played by the rule, in other words, you've never been sexually involved with anybody since birth, that you are automatically free from going through hardship, and challenging times once you are married. This law in of itself does not change the law of nature by allowing you to live simultaneously in this world of problems of all sort, chaos, diseases, and death, and yet at the same time you will never be affected by them. It is impossible, but what it does for you is that you don't have to deal with its consequence in that you've set precedence for a good life until the end, and if anything should happen to you during the course of your life, you will not be held accountable because you did not open the door, and you will not be judged for anything, and ultimately you won't be guilty of breaking the law something you should be proud about.

Unlike those who've broken the law numerous times, would have to deal with the guilt in their conscience for the rest of their lives, where they would have to face judgment because of being disobedient. As I often say to my daughter about breaking the law, that terrible things always happen to those who disobey. It is a manner from my part as parent to draw her attention to choose to do well, even during suffering, and pain to make sure that she understands that it also makes sense that good things always happen to those who obey. The fact of the matter is, reward always follows good works versus punishment for evildoing. The quality of life that one must hope to have begins primarily in the first step of obedience in life.

Since you've come out your mother's womb, you've been told to obey, respect, and honor your parents for it is good for you. If for instance you have received from your parents up to the point where you are grown enough to make up your mind about things in life, and you've not broken the first law in your life, you are most likely to follow through with other matters in life such as sexual relationship. The same is true if you've broken the first commandment you are going to break other laws that matter much in life, because you've set precedence in that direction, and you can rest assured that terrible things will happen to you unfortunately. For there is such a thing about laws in general in every person's life that is once guilty of one, you are guilty of all because the first one always opens the door for the others to follow.

It is my belief that the generation of the 21st century has the greatest potential ever than any previous generations to promote wellness by keeping up a higher standard that leads to a high quality of education, great family values, financially secured, excellent health care benefits, great source of renewable energy, good life of environmental protection, strong moral conviction to live, and ultimately a higher regard for the natural laws to uphold in a society that simply cannot stop from going deeper down in the abyss of sexual perversion and immorality.

The generations that come before our generation did not have so much as far as technologies, infrastructures, and other means necessary to spread out the rich and ideal standards that have kept their society in checks and balances when it came to morality, conviction, respect for the law of the land, character, and social environmental protection. They did what they had to do to be busy to make it a goal upon themselves so that they would see another day better than the day before whether socially, economically, morally without trying to destroy lives by using humans lives as means to an end unlikely the way we are doing things today in our midst. They have been steadfast as their great grandparents had been in keeping the moral laws within their families, workplaces, and the society entirely as they should, because they needed to do so for us, to appreciate their arduous work, in honoring them by following their examples they left.

Unfortunately, we have failed them both their hard works and their lives they had sacrificed to leave a legacy to promote a better life for ourselves and for our children and grandchildren to come. If they were to have a chance to live in our days and to see what we have done with their works they had left us, they would certainly be perturbed and appalled beyond human understanding, and they would be totally sad over the fact that they had sacrificed to give us so much better than they had, they would regret it forever. So, we need not to live for ourselves as we have been doing in almost every aspect of our lives, we need to stop and see the big picture before us so that our lives would not be an instrument of destruction, but rather an element of service and encouragement to make our world better as we are looking forward to abiding by the law established around us, and to support the effort of our forefathers in continuing the legacy in a traditional way, so that we can be morally strong, developing convictions, having strong character to abstain from all sort of sexual immoralities, and preparing the way of good life for the future generation free from guilt and regret.

May this be every man and every woman's goal to realize with hope before departing from this world, knowing in their heart they leave this world with something to contribute in making a difference for a change not to contribute to destroy it! And with that kind of resolve within the conscience of every individual on the face of this planet, it would in fact kill this venomous poison ideology to believe that it is ok to be sexually involved at any time. Yes! It is ok, but not that ok as you would imagine. It is ok when we all realize both those of us who are practically involved and who are not before marriage, to respect the directives concerning sexual relationship within people as we stand to follow the steps that lead to such act where we would not have to choose to violate our conscience, in pursuing a relationship where love can prevail instead being in it just for sexual pleasure.

THE SEX FACTOR

In every home in the United States of America, and certainly in every home around the world without exception each family must deal in a unique way the reality of sexuality as it relates to human race in part. The crucial point of such reality of our culture is governed by an enormous disrespect among the sexes and certain entities of our society that creates uproar where morality is being put on the sideline to destabilize social structure for sexual involvement. It has been for centuries the agenda of many that one-day sexuality would be the ideal etiquette in the market, presented in many forms with the intent to transform the reality of every individual life upon the earth. That is the reason why, it is of no surprise at all that we are seeing such impatience among the young people not to wait, and a lack of discernment from the adults to vaguely encourage and promote sexual activities, if it brings pleasure and lucrativeness for their enrichment, they can be careless morally speaking for the welfare of the society. The question is why do people of the earth fill up with greed for such a thing? It has become epidemic to the point that the life of the humans revolves around it. It looks as if there is a desperate need for it for everyone to be involved in regardless of age.

Frankly, the enthusiasm there is in engaging in such activity on a regular basis is astronomical compare it to, if you will, a single day blood drive to save lives. It should have been more compelling for many to donate blood for a greater cause, to do so with a better enthusiasm and to be optimistic about it, because the result of anybody donating blood is rather ethical without judging the source, which in effect will be used for the benefit of saving another life than to be part of something not only is unethical, but also at the same time gives way to countless eventual woes of life. Friends it ought not to be so among us human beings, sex is frankly a small act, and yet, it can do serious damages in a society when it is being controlled by it. The sex factor as you would call it is deadly when it is used contrarily from its proper context, which is marriage only.

It has been reported repeatedly in the news that many official public servants have been brought down because of sexual scandals. We've seen government official such as governors, senators, mayors, commissioners, presidential candidates have come forward to apologize to their constituents and their families because of their inappropriate sexual encounters. We also had in the past sitting President of the United States of America and I am sure many more around the world who have been brought before the world to give explanation concerning their sexual behavior, where they had to apologize for it.

Furthermore, and very unfortunate, there has been series of sexual scandals among those who supposedly are called to be morally strong such are pastors, evangelists, priests, and so forth, even now the worst of all many churches now opening their doors to so called opened gay, and lesbian bishops. So now, where is it that the line should be drawn? You mean to think that church would have been the last place on earth you would hear such a thing. This sex thing has become so much out of control that people begin to question, is there such a thing as morality anymore? What do you think?

In the book titled "Safer sex the new morality" the author Evelyn Lerman has put together testimonies of people who have things to say about sex, here are some personal testimonies:[1] a woman named Nana Jeanne, a great grand-mother of 11, she was born in 1897 and died in 1999, she said in her own words "you must remember that in my day when I was growing up as a teenager, we did not know about sex".

Wow! This must be surprising for you to notice that she did not know about sex in her days as oppose to ours. Perhaps she was purposefully aware that girls, or kids of her age should in no way be involved in such relation, something that was only for married couples as it related to her upbringing in the society. She goes on to say that "When the girls got together in a group they say to each other, where do babies come from?" It was all they knew about sex, she said "it was something I had to do for my husband (sex)".

Miss Nana lived to be more than 100 years old, she lived long enough to have noticed that we people of the late 20th and early 21st centuries have brought problems and woes of life upon ourselves deliberately as results of how we conduct ourselves sexually, she said.

"I really don't know why the young teenagers in the late fifties and sixties went so free and wild. It was probably because society brought so much to their attention – sex, pornography, movies – all encouraging them in their desire for freedom. But I think it's on the wane, I really do".

There was another testimonial from the same book of a wonderful lady by the name of Ula. She was in the year of 1911; she had the opportunity to go to college at the time when young women of her age would not have the privilege. She and many of young ladies did not partake of sex while she spent her junior year in college in France because it was illegal to display contraceptives in pharmacies in the 1920's in the state of Connecticut, and that was then she learned about them (the pills). Here's what she said about her life regarding sex then:

"we had sex education at home from our mother, but the teachers were too shy to talk about sex in school. I went to my first dance when I was 13".

Of course, they were to be transported to the place there by their parents since they could not drive themselves and were not allowed to do so then. As far as the party was, she went on to say "all parties were chaperoned …. In high school, we went to dances and we necked and petted. Necking was rather restrained, and petting was a bit more involved" she said: "in college we had to sign out and say exactly where we were going".

Oh boy! How is that for our today's colleges to require students to specify their whereabouts while they are there? This would be taken way out of proportion, but the fact is we all can learn something good from the past and exercise it in our lives today.

And she also said "we protected our friends by signing them

out for the night and saying they were going to a friend's house. Actually, they were in a neighboring town with a boyfriend. I never heard anyone getting pregnant, and there were no babies".

Many colleges offer courses regarding human anatomy in a very pervasive way, but Ula had things differently back then in a very conservative way, she said "it wasn't until I got to college that I was offered science, only the boys had science in high school. Freshman in college we had hygiene 101, and that's when we were introduced to our bodies. Most of us were still ignorant about the actual means of reproduction".

Miss Ula was "very close to her mother" she said, she mentioned that she did not know much about young men. She graduated from high school at the age of 19 but couldn't attend Yale because of discrimination against women; they were not allowed to be admitted there then. Besides, when she was at Smith she said "we heard rumors about a group of women who lived in a particular wing in a special dormitory. There were whispers about them, so we were aware of homosexual, of lesbians and gay men". I suspect such lifestyle was immoral, to the point of those, who engaged themselves that way, were ashamed of it, they had to be in the hiding. Miss Ula continued her experiences as a young lady back then she said "when I was a young woman, even in Europe, there were always chaperones at a party.

Now I really don't know". She is in her 90's "there is no chaperoning; I think teens shouldn't have sex at least until college because they were too immature, too irresponsible, too young to know the consequences. We need better sex education; we need to teach responsibility; our whole moral texture is so different today. We are missing something in our whole way of life. I wouldn't want to provide contraception to the very young even through clinics. There should be more education even for the parents, by the schools, the churches and the temples, so they would know how to teach their children. Now they are not watching them, not teaching them. Maybe we don't have to talk too much about morality, but we can sure talk about responsibility". Regardless of what generation you grew up from, we all have something unique, and special to say about "sex" and we dealt with it whether socially, privately, ethically, politically, religiously.[2]

I certainly appreciate the testimonies of those who've come before us in sharing perspectives on how it was for them growing up in the 20's, 40's, 60's and so forth. They have had great successes and unfortunately some failures, which strengthened them to become the persons they were and to have the courage to share with our generation what we ought to do, or not, so that we can maintain a culture of healthy living without compromising those principles that are clearly given to us to follow in context of our sexual conduct of everyday life. We ought to know that there are boundaries we should respect when it comes to sexual life both inwardly and outwardly. We do not need to make it hard on ourselves, nor do we need to make it a matter of personal issue in seeking our right, or the freedom to choose to act foolishly.

It is not about you, or anything else of this planet earth, but it is rather about the one who gave us His principles to follow concerning life in general, and about every single aspect of it according to His word. It is in fact wise of each one of us to comply with His will in obedience to His word which we will come to do the hard way instead of disobeying it. My hope is that every young boy and every young girl, or every one of us on the face of the planet earth comes to realization that we are indeed in subjection to the authority of the creator, and that we need to accept His lordship no matter what. Can it be excited to submit to His lordship? Yes! Indeed, it can, it all depends on how you respond to it. If you choose to respond to submission to Him, He will lead you to peace, prosperity, freedom, and happiness, but if you choose otherwise, the woes of life will be on you every step of the way, and your destiny will be totally ruined.

For this reason, our sexual desires should not be motives by which we purposely, or perhaps involuntarily stand in the way of the creator's principles to live our lives in relationship with others romantically. We don't need to let sex, or to allow it to be the definer of our lives in which everything we say and do should be associated with such.

In fact, it ought to be our goal that we should be defined by a set of values that uphold truth, the sanctity of human life, a higher standard which governs our lives that leads to peace, prosperity, and happiness instead of wasting our lives to pursue vain desires in accomplishing works that will be detrimental for other human lives which apparently may seem to be lucratively ok. Yes! It is good to share our lives with others, but not in the way that is morally wrong, and certainly not in the way where our sexual conduct can be used as weapons to endanger other lives we suppose to protect.

With that in mind, let's reason within ourselves to arrive with a single conclusion to acknowledge that we have been given the gift of life, so we should in no way jeopardize it with our sexual selfish desires that lift immorality to be a model to uphold within our society. May we be afraid and scared to realize that each time we falter, we are becoming agents of sowing evil seeds in the field of the minds of our people of our society, which will eventually destroy them if not sooner, but later anyway. We've got to exercise courage to say no to what appear to be fun, nice to have, sensual in nature, even to the freedom to choose evil instead of good for a fleeting moment of pleasure, when it is we face the challenge to make the best of it, in the benefit of everyone around for the better. This is what we need to do, for which we were created, to have a culture of life in a plain level of field, where our motives are pure before each other in seeking to support marriage relationship between a man and a woman without changing the nature of the fundamental principles by which men and women are called to come together romantically.

Unfortunately, however, there are those with their perverted liberal minds who will continue to press on spreading the advocacy of a pluralistic agenda within our society, which will promote the homosexual lifestyle, the gay and lesbian manifesto, we need to personally stand against such apparatus to defend that which was given to us since the beginning of time regarding romantic relationship. We need to pay very close attention to things that we embrace to be part of our lives on a regular basis. Such things like books we read, the movies that we watch, people's ideas, or philosophies that we listen to, or even sermons we listen to at church, so that we won't find ourselves to become accustomed to something that is not legally a problem, but at the same time morally wrong. Remember we are creatures that need constant change in our lives, it is not a bad idea that we make good inventory in our lives, in measuring it to the highest standard of the Almighty, He alone is sovereign, He alone is powerful, we should never second guess His will and never again to stand in His way as He is dealing with us to change us in and out, to make us better as He is pleased.

As we are dealing with these vicious, if not deadly elements in this book that are threatening our lives, I hope that you will always remember that the emphasis is not as much on you as it is on "The creator". The reason for it all, is because His sovereignty over us all, gives Him the ultimate authority over our lives to demand whatever His heart desires. His sovereignty makes Him no respecter of person, He demands total surrender, and in other words He owns you. Perhaps you are saying if this is the way He wants things, it certainly makes Him a dangerous dictator. No, His standard does not make Him a dictator, but God and since He is God He is not operated the same by our limitations to think and to act as human beings do, the only creatures on the earth that disobey Him, in other words, we leave the path that He puts us in to go our own way contrary to His character and His holiness.

In almost every aspect of our lives we stand in contradiction before God. For examples, in government we should have understood that it was designed to be a representation of the triune God: God the Father, God the Son, God the Holy Spirit. Unfortunately, we make it something of our own, in orchestrating all kinds of corruption in all its branches.

In church, we almost completely wipe out the great traditions, and the ordinances that have passed unto us from our forefathers, the patriarchs of the faith, to embrace contemporary liberal and socialistic approach, while church supposed to be a lighthouse for its community, a spiritual refuge for the afflicted and the oppressed, and as well as an embassy for God's kingdom on earth.

Not only that, we have family, an institution designed by God as a nucleus to continue the legacy that He once started with the first family in the Garden of Eden. This institution was supposed to be a place of training to continue to grow, in knowing God's purpose, to prepare citizens to obey God to respect government, and to live peaceably with others in the community. Since order has been destroyed in the home, it destroys man's morality as well totally, where his conscience is seared partly against the affair of God's kingdom, and toward God himself. To make matters worse, he rebels toward His creator and another way to express his hatred toward God besides government, church, and family, is his sexuality. He simply cannot appreciate the design that was made for him, which is mankind was created male and female and that they were to join in sacred matrimony where the man should leave his mother and his father to cleave unto his wife intended by God, whereas they have joined together let no man put asunder.[4] This sentiment of hatred toward God has driven man to make his sexuality a factor that questions God's sovereignty in the effort to dethrone God, and ultimately to kill Him (**Gen. 2:24**).

Needless to say, this effort has been tried before to no avail while Lucifer was particularly being after God's throne in heaven, and consequently he was evicted from there forever and condemned to be cast in the lake of fire for all eternity. Therefore, he is not happy, he is raging a battle against God, and the only way he thinks he is going to win this battle, is by turning God's creation, us human beings, our hearts against Him, so that we in turn can be in the same place that awaits him some day, because he knows God is

Holy, if we are not clean like He is, we cannot partake in His kingdom.

Unfortunately, some people believe that, and that is why they are trying so hard to measure up to God's standard, and they give up so easily because they believe they cannot ever make it to God, that is the devil's plan to make you believe that, there is no way you can make it to God no matter what you do. Yes, that is true in part for the fact you can never make it to God in your own way, but they also forget that God has made a way for you and me to come to Him, and that way is "Jesus Christ" His only begotten Son that He gave on the cross of Calvary there to pay the sin's debt of the whole wide world (**John 14:6; John 3: 16**).

By the way the debt has been paid in full for all of us human beings, we don't owe a thing to God, and certainly not the devil for that matter, all we have to do is to only accept the gift of salvation that God provided for us through his Son Jesus, and once we do that, it will put the devil and his fallen angels and the demons out of their misery in hell for ever where they belong, for this place was created only for them not for us.

Yet at the same time unfortunately, the devil and his demons will win you if you resist God's way of salvation, you will find yourself in the same place with them. My friend, the only way you will be able to have complete victory over the devil is to accept God's plan for your life beginning with putting your trust in Jesus Christ for salvation and the rest to follow, but if you don't, you continue to listen to your wisdom even though you may not like the devil and not even involved in his things, or not listening to him, you will end up the same place with him, because your only ticket out is to trust Jesus as your Lord and Savior in your heart, that's what I did and that's what you should do too. My friend, for as long as you live on this earth, your life can never be better even though you may possess everything there is, because on the other side of life which is death, that's where it all begins, because death is not the end is the beginning of life eternal in another dimension, and that's the most important part.

In effect, when you accept Jesus by asking him to come into your heart to save you, what happens though, your name is automatically written in the book of life registry in heaven by God, even though you're still alive, technically you are in heaven because first of all that's all it takes to get there, second of all this is your reservation that secures your place there upon your death, the moment you depart the planet earth and find yourself there as soon as you open your eyes.

As oppose to hell you do not need to accept anybody, or to put your trust on anyone for that matter, it is automatic if you <u>don't accept Jesus as your Lord and Savior</u> your destination was already the lake of fire. Please understand that it is not up to God to decide for you. Your eternal destination, in fact it is all up to you because you're the one who will determine that. Failure to do so, you will be there in hell as soon as you open your eyes after death as well, but my friend you do not have to go there, the devil does not want you to know that, and that's all the reason he is trying to occupy your mind, your time with all things of this world, so that when your time on this earth is over, you will miss the opportunity to meet <u>Jesus as your Lord and Savior</u>, but assuredly as your judge.

Please understand, the devil has no power over you except God, but he can trick you to believe otherwise and to make you do things that you will regret for the rest of your life. Friend; listen to me, take it from someone who's been there in the paws of the devil himself, but God miraculously has saved not only my soul, but also saved me from the hands of the devil. So, you see, the devil is not only taking advantage of your life and your time in encouraging you to live out your sexuality in any way shape, or form possible against the character of God Almighty, but also, he is buying himself some time knowing what's awaiting him ahead to get as many as people like you and me to believe on his cause in distracting you from seeing God's goodness so that you can be with him in hell.

Notice friend, it is not because you are practicing homosexuality, or being involved in any sexual immorality that automatically sends you to hell as you're probably come to believe, <u>but the one and only reason a person goes to hell, is because that person has never accepted Jesus as his Lord</u> and Savior. **Therefore, he goes to hell for the fact that the only ticket he had for heaven was Jesus, but he never accepted him.** The same the only way a person goes to heaven is not because he was not involved in any sexual immorality, or because he was kind, moral, or perhaps he was living a good and clean life. No! Friend, <u>it was only because he had put his trust in Jesus for salvation that was the only reason.</u> Make no mistake friend, when it comes to heaven and hell and who goes here and there, is not done on the basis who's good, or bad, or who's done honorable deeds, or evil, but it is done only based on who is **obedient to God regarding His Son Jesus Christ for salvation.**

So, this idea of you deciding to do whatever you please with your life put you in direct contact with the devil himself to work together, in trying to destroy the work of God. Such behaviors like homosexuality, pornography, prostitution, fornication, adultery, masturbation, or any other type of sexual perversion out there are the devil's ways to keep you from experiencing God's wonderful blessings in your life, in wasting your life to do the devil's will who (God) will ultimately destroy both your life and your soul.

This sex factor is our way to show to which we belong to, whether we are for God, or we are for the devil. If we are God's we will listen to Him and if our life reflects something different from His standard, then we'll know who our father is. We cannot serve two masters at the same time, we've got to make it a goal to truly come to a point of our life to say we are indeed God's, and so we will act like it, and if we are not, we should stay away and not being a hindrance for his creation, but let's be an asset for Him to spread out His word, and when we do that little by little we are causing people to leave the kingdom of darkness to come to the kingdom of light, where morality prevails always.

Something that I have always bothered by over the years regarding the sex factor when it comes to parents, to what they ought to be for their children, they instead become their body in harboring the wrong kind of sexual examples, in using them to influence their children to practice the so called "safe sex". I wonder in their mind what are they thinking? Since we've discussed it before in that line of thinking, that it is only when a person marries that's when he/she is ready, and free to have fully <u>sexual intercourse</u> according to the words of the Almighty God (**Gen. 2: 24**). Truly a person may not be ready to be sexually active mentally, or emotionally before, or even after marriage, but such is not the premise that is given to be sexually active. That is the reason why, I am so appalled for the fact, that I have listened to parents' testimonies that they do not have any problem for their teenage kids to be sexually active only if they can finish high school first, or perhaps if they know they are ready for it.

Here are testimonies of stayed home parents of two teenage kids 15 and 13 who are having conflict between two sets of principles about comprehensive sexuality education, and abstinence only. Let's meet "Julie and Jim" from the book "Safer sex The New Morality".[5]

"What do you want your teenagers to know about sexuality?"

Julie answered "I feel they should know a lot and I want them to have a positive attitude. I don't want them to feel pushed into sex when they aren't ready for it. I like to keep the lines of communication open. Sex is a wonderful thing when you're ready, not when you're not".

"What should schools be teaching in sexuality education classes?"

"Julie: we have a great program here that begins in fifth grade. Some parents thought that it was too early, but I think it's perfect. They are old enough to retain information; it catches them before they begin to develop. Schools can get into feelings during freshman year in high school"

"At what age do you think it's appropriate for teens to have sex?"

"Julie: I'm kind of conservative about that. I told my daughter I'd like her to wait until college. Her mind and body will develop more after high school".

"Do you think parents can make a difference?"

"Julie: Definitely, they need to let children know they remember their feelings when they were growing up. They need to form parents' networks. Parents need to let each other know how they feel about curfews, things like that. Parents need to be with their kids, drive them around, listen to what they talk about, get to know their friends, bring up subjects with them. They need to give their opinions on things".

"Jim: parents get report cards. They work with their children from birth to puberty and beyond, and then the day comes when the young person goes out and does things on her/his own. They come back with body piercing, but they come back okay. The parents get a b+. But you're still doing fine. The fear factor isn't a terrible thing either. I mean letting your children know that their reputations depend on their behavior. The labels are out there in high school. If you're loose especially girls, it gets out and you're labeled. It can't hurt for them to worry about that".

"What about the media? What role should they have?"

"Julie: They could have public service announcements about sexually transmitted infections, but it's hard to put condoms on a billboard! I get conflicted because on the one hand you want to be open, understanding and approachable. On the other hand, you don't want to push them into sex before they're ready. Well maybe the billboards would be all right. I guess it is ok".[6]

I do appreciate both "Jim and Julie's" testimonies for this segment, but unfortunately, I do have a problem with her approach concerning the timing she thinks her kids can get sexually involved. I believe that she is truly sincere when she said: "I told my daughter I 'd like her to wait until college" meaning to have sexual intercourse. I would like to ask her on what ground or authority she stands on to counsel her daughter that way? Because in my opinion she has a wrong view of sexual relationship since the premise for someone to begin sexual engagement is not on a conventional timing, but rather on a specific principle given by God Himself.

Furthermore, I am not sure that "Julie" understood the idea of being ready for sexual intercourse because if she did, she would have thought anybody of any age can have free reign to have sex at any time regardless their age, if they are ready even the small kids. I sincerely believe until we have a good grasp and a firm conviction about sexual relationship to know that it is only through marriage relationship for such act to occur, we will always get it wrong no matter how you feel about this subject every time you talk about it, teach it, encourage it, and even involve in it. Let it be known unto you that sexual relationship is not about mankind's desire to seek to fulfill it, but it's all about the creator's will regardless your feelings, wants, desires, and others. When God created you, He did it with all the needs and desires you would have in mind. That's why you have them, but He wants you to access those desires within the parameter of a marriage relationship between a man and a woman only. Once you adhere to this fundamental principle of such relationship, you are not in violation with Him, and then we will all be protected, and spared at the judgment's day. (*Not at the last day*)

CHAPTER 4

THE PERVERSION OF SEX

At last we all must agree on something, that human beings are greatly involved in all kinds of sexual behaviors, which in turn destroy the proper context of love, relationship, and intimacy. We are in a world of tolerance and moral relativism which simply gives way to choices where right and wrong become automatically a matter of preference, which consequently crumbles society to a level worse than animal beings. For this cause, it has been apparent within the society that man is in search for freedom, a freedom yet at the same time enslaves him because he is not accepting the fact that he has no rights over anything, but only privileges. This notion of privilege causes many to grind their teeth, to beat up their chest because this idea according to them seems number one, to assume responsibility.

Secondly it makes them look like people who are looking for favor, and since they only give orders, favor is not an option for them. Of course, asking for favor, there is nothing wrong with that, it simply shows the condition of one's heart, the humility that allows him to submit himself under a government and other kinds of authority over him without complaining. Realistically speaking a person of such nature is very prideful to say the least, because it is not in his nature to follow direction except when it is convenience to his benefits, not only that he will make a simple matter to become a situation almost impossible to resolve just to satisfy his narcissistic ego above everybody else regardless the damages that he may inflict to others[1]. Therefore, such individual will do all it takes to acquire leverage and economic power to rally some significant percentage of the society to follow his view, to prosper even though his view may not be at best a cause to influence others, to stir up society, he will keep at it just for the sake of being annoying, or rebellious toward authority, he will still maintain his agenda.

So imagine, if there be such a person in the society with a perverted mind that represents not much in the society, but if we were to multiply that same individual by a thousand, as a result of that we multiply that thousand by another thousand, so now we have thousands upon thousands of people like minded in the society that set out to influence other thousands of people which eventually will corrupt the same society that was once safe, protected to become a society of perverted minds that is bound to be destroyed with a rapid flow, even though the obvious was simply to adhere by the norms. In fact, with that kind of mindset, it won't be long before you begin to see an increase of immorality within the society, mainly around sexual activities, which will give ways to homosexuality, promiscuity, prostitution, lesbianism, adultery, fornication, extramarital affairs, bestiality, and lots of other kind of sexual perversion that destroy lives.

Perhaps many would argue that it does not really matter which way to take with your sexual life, it will all come down to one thing only that is "we all are going to die". The point of being walking away from involving in any sexual lifestyle is ludicrous, for no matter what you do you cannot keep yourself from thinking of sexual thoughts, let alone not involving in them since they are available to us 24 hrs a day. The way the world is going right now, it seems as if almost impossible that one would timidly avoid having any contact with the ambiance of the world, where morally teenagers would not smoke at all at least when they turn 20, but they do now at the earliest possible, even at 12 and 13 years old.

WHY GUILT . . . . AFTER SEX

They would not normally go to strip clubs, parties for fear of being adducted or raped; now they do, and because of that, we are seeing more and more kids' drunk and driven cars under the influence, and consequently over all, they are sexually involved, they do drugs, and they are having babies prematurely. And so therefore, life seems to be unfair to them they would rebel to anything that would stand in their way, according to them they are none sense, they are only a bunch of rules that hold them from having fun.

Here are some examples of sexual perversion that are present among us in the society.

When it comes to homosexuality once again sex has been perverted, the principle has been violated for the fact that it is strictly forbidden by the creator of all things that two people of the same gender to participate in a sexual way. It is explicitly an act of disobedience from man toward the principle established regarding such behavior. This type of action in entertaining a relationship between two individuals of the same sex is not normal for the continuity of life of a human being. It is making the nature of life to go against the nature, the sanctuary whereby we have been placed to live, because the environment we know of as the planet earth, we are not given the permission to live outside of it. This is the only place humans were born to live collectively as a people.

Therefore, we do not have the authority to change the natural way of living in an environment that is unique for human being to decide whether to co-habit in like manner man with man or woman with woman. This so called same sex relationship is not normal to the very core of the fundamental principle of human creation. The abnormality of such relationship is not in the desire to choose whom you want to be with, and it is not even in the name of love for that matter, but it is rather a voice, the voice of the creator that says: "It is an abomination before me regarding human creation to live that way" (**Leviticus 20 : 13; Romans 1 : 18-32**).[2]

However, it would be perfectly normal for two individuals of the same sex to love and to live together for the rest of their lives, if we were to apply this saying "man is the measure of all things" that, the reality of a kind of relationship would have been ideal just for the fact that man would be the ultimate authority. Unfortunately, it is a lie, man is not the measure of all things, man is not the creator, but rather a creature. He is a created being that first needs to learn to show reverence to the creator as his authority. Second, because his creator has the authority over him, He has the right to tell him what to do, and what not to do, and his responsibility is to obey Him fully. So, you see my friend, it is not a matter of choice, or preference, it is a matter of principle that you and I need to adhere to, just to be obedient to the one that created everything even us human beings. Our life should not be a mockery as it reflects His image, so that He can be pleased in everything we say and do. The question to you is, is it normal for two individuals of the same gender to be romantically involved? The answer is no! no, because it is not up to you to decide, but rather to abide, or obey the one that has the ultimate authority over you and over everything there is, if not, there will be consequences following your disobedience toward the principle that He wants you to comply with according to His will.

Friend think about it, there is no mystery behind the principle when it comes to sexual relationship; it is in our best interest that we should seek to obey the principle instead of ignoring it, because our life depends upon our willingness to obey, regardless how we may feel about it. Why one should go to that road? Many would continue to practice this lifestyle, even though they can clearly see the revealed power of God through creation, because they have a defiant nature, they do not want God to rule over them.[3] In the natural way, we notice that anything that connects, or links one thing to another follows the principle of heterosexual relationship. That is: there is one that represents the male gender and the other the female gender. For example, if anybody need to use any type of electrical appliances, the appliance that is being used should be plugged in the power source. The image there is, the appliance is always going to be the male portion and the power source is always in fact the female portion. When the two items come together, there is in effect a relationship between two opposite genders so to speak, in other words the two become one and continue to be so until they are disconnected from each other.

You see friend there is nothing magical about that, it is only natural, and normal, because of the fact, this is the only way to bring about two opposite connectors when it comes to appliances, or two people of the opposite sexes if you will, to become one in a relationship which by the way is being done within the parameter of sexual principle given by the creator. No one can dare say "I don't like that principle when it comes to appliances, I am going to do it my way, and I am going to connect two appliances, or two other items of the same kind and nature together". You know what, it does not work that way, no matter how much anybody would love to make two appliances of the same nature to work, it will never, because the reason for it is simple. The maker of the appliance made it to be operable according to the sexual principle that brings a male connector to a female connector together.

Besides, the connector male from an appliance, or any other types of electrical devices would never say, or will ever say one day, they want electrical appliances rights, they don't want to connect any more to a female power source, they want their makers to only connect them with male connector otherwise they will not render services to places such as: restaurants, hotels, kitchen homes etc. There ought to be laws written to protect same gender connector rights, and they would ask congress from the electricity' world to amend the appliance's constitution to give them equal rights and protect their lifestyle in the world of electrical devices. Can you understand the silliness of this statement concerning an electric appliance? if you can understand it, imagine how much, much more unreasonable it is for human beings to consider two people of the same gender to be together as a couple living in a natural way, and on top of that demand to amend the constitution for equal rights as normal as a heterosexual couple's rights. This is outrageous! The maker of appliances would not budge to respond to the demand of his works. Why would the creator do otherwise to His creation? Can you honestly answer truthfully this question to say that the creature has the right to decide how to live his life before his creator? I think the obvious is not at all! In fact, there is no way this can ever happen because the principle is there to obey it, not to amend it, or replace it, since it was given by the creator Himself. Deal with it! Obviously not in a combative way because God is merciful, He will show grace to all.

Understand that the lesson we're sharing in using the homosexual example with the hope to draw your attention to the reality that in fact this kind of behavior is indeed abnormal. There is no intention whatsoever to demean the personality of homosexual representatives, but truthfully to engage in a series of teaching with the hope to bring light to those who sincerely believe that it is up to them to decide the direction of their lives at the expense of destroying more lives, and to fulfill their heart's desire in making it to be a way of life.

In fact, there is nothing wrong with people who are homosexual as human beings, because they were fearfully and wonderfully made by the creator (**Ps. 139: 14**).[4] Nothing absolutely nothing is wrong with them, but the abnormality is in the way they choose to live the life that was given to them, since the day they were conceived in their mother's womb. The problem with such life is because it is against the natural way of life; it is devilish even to the core, where the real reason about such ideology is to undermine the foundation of why we were created, and to destroy the very existence of the entire human race on the planet earth. A normal way of life will never entertain the possibility of destroying human lives. The point here is, remember earlier I said that anybody who is in violation of the law, in other words to stand against the natural law of life, is in effect putting one's life on the line, because homosexuality is one of the tools in this world presented to human as an alternative lifestyle to contemplate, but, it kills instead of improving human life.

Make no mistake about it, when it gets a hold of a human life, it is bound to destroy, it is to bring society to a place of confusion regarding who they are in dealing with their sexuality contrarily to the way we were born to live as individuals. The damage is always from the part of an alternate lifestyle, not from the original one that was traditionally given to us from a mom and a dad point of view family unit. The individual, who is in favor of the homosexual lifestyle, is not practically a bad person just because he chooses this path of life; he only makes a wrong choice which he will have to deal with the consequences resulted from his choice.

My intention please is not to put down anybody in any way who chooses to go that route to find fulfillment. My intention, however, is to educate from a natural stand point that this path of life will put the homosexual practices lifestyle in conflict with his natural being (gender) also with the purpose for which he was created. It is not by any stretch of imagination that my intention is neither to condemn anybody who is in this lifestyle, nor at the same time I am trying to condone this lifestyle, for I know that I know it is wrong, not only for anybody to consider it, or a society entirely to embrace it, but also it is simply wrong said the creator, period (**Leviticus 20: 13; Romans 1: 18-32**).

I have written this section of the book very respectfully to those whom it may be a concern of such lifestyle, not to revolutionize against their lifestyle, and not because I am looking for a fight, but because out of an expression of love that I want to point out the danger, in an effort to avoid it at all cost, since I am also a member of this planet, so I feel strongly that it is my responsibility to engage this society head on to flee this life and the temptation of it before it is too late. I do not want to tell anybody how to live his life, the choice is not mine, I can only account for myself, but it is always good to have a little reminder every once and awhile, so that the normalcy of life as it intended to be can prevail within the society for the betterment of humanity.

Meanwhile, when things are getting out of hands within the society, it affects every human life one way, or another, that is why when I speak about, or against this subject, it is my way of contributing to the betterment of the society, whereby I have the right and the privilege to serve. It is as well as mine your responsibility to work to the benefit of one another, in embracing the norms that keep the society going in the right direction, and to purposely decide to do good, good not to practice evil, or anything that is evil based such as homosexuality, each time the opportunity comes our way.

With that in mind, we need to be careful as to what we want to teach our children to be right and wrong. It is important to them and as well as to us parents that they know whatever they end up doing in life, or become, it is not by default of some random coincidence occurrence, but because they know with factual discoveries, that it is what it is without uncertainty, where they will not juggle two ideas in hoping to make the right choice. It does really matter of what it is that you are trying to do in life, because it involves people, it will influence some for better, for worse, or for good, and some for evil. Which side you want to be in influencing others, do you want to influence for evil, or for good? My encouragement to you is to stand on the side that helps influence others for good. Homosexuality is not a good influence among our race, but evil, for this reason you ought to stay away from it, and it is also a form of sexual perversion.

To enjoy your life freely, the way it ought to be, is to get rid of all wrong kinds of human behavior, or lifestyle for that matter homosexuality, so that you can experience real freedom to the fullness. For those of you who are already involved in such a lifestyle, you need to come out of it very fast, because it is for your own good to do so, and for the benefit of others. It is not about when homosexuality is being presented as evil, for it is evil, in fact it is about something that is greater than we, whose none of us have no right to decide on the matter, but to just obey and follow directions.

Now what about an individual who genuinely believes this is the life that has been given to him and without it his life will never be the same, and he loves it because he makes him feel good about himself, and about everything else in life. He also believes that there is nothing abnormal about this lifestyle, if others cannot see that, or accept him the way he is, that's their problem, they need to deal with it, and not to stick their noses to where they don't belong. What would you say to an individual like that?

First, I would say that he is right that without this lifestyle his life will never be the same instead it will be normal, safer, healthier, and better. Second, to live a lifestyle such as homosexuality was not given to him, he simply allowed himself to be drawn to it, and in other word, he made a conscientious choice to live such a life because of his world view of life. His world view is exactly that "Man is the measure of all things" he believes that he has the right to choose to become whoever he wants, and that it is only his business not anybody's else to decide for him whether, or not to be what he wants to be. For example, he believes that it is solely his right to decide to die his hair black, or white, or any color for that matter, he does not think that he needs to abide by any law, or to any authority to do so. Therefore, his mentality, or his perspective on things becomes his law that guides him to do whatever he wants, so that he does not have to answer to anybody following his actions upon his life. Furthermore, he feels threatened and intimidated by those who think they are better than he and dare to tell him that he has no right upon his own life, for that he sees it as a violation of invading his privacy.

However, his life will never be the same if his world view were his life was created by the creator of all things, and that He is the one that has the right over his life not him, in fact the creator can say this is normal, this is not so, that He is the one that gives directions and instructions that lead us to a better life, because

He has the sovereignty to do so. His lifestyle would not be the opposite of the creator's will, but instead in perfect harmony with it. Because of his worldview of life in general, he has no reverence for authority, he believes that he was not created he is simply a product of evolution, he came from monkey, he is not responsible for his actions, he is simply acting upon his natural being as a descendant of a specie that has no concept of right and wrong, for that we just have to tolerate him just like he is, and learn to live with him regardless of his action just like he has to deal with ours in a world where everybody has rights to do, or decide whatever they want to do with their life.

For this reason, how dare us to interfere with his life the way it is, and to tell him that it is not normal. It will always be like that when individuals are confused about their sexual identity, or their reality, because they do not want to acknowledge that there are principles that govern this life, and behind them there is also a lawgiver who purposely seeks His way into the affair of mankind regardless of our willingness to obey Him or not.

With that in mind, we as human beings are not products of the theory of evolution, but rather of creation, that is the reason why it is not up to man to decide, or to make amends as to how this life should live, or the question should be: who's got the authority to say what's right and what's wrong? It ought to be to us that we are not interfering with the creator's business instead of concerning what this individual from this end, or the other thinks. No one has the authority over anything except it was given by the creator, not even over his own life, you do not have the authority, because of the fact you are not the author of it, you are simply a steward, which by the way, one day you will give an account about your life of what you did with it whether good, or evil.[5]

Homosexuality is one of them; make a good assessment of your life, if you have used it for homosexuality purposes, because you are surely going to stand before the judge, the author of life. Friend the reality that everybody decides what to do and what not to do with his life is perfectly understandable, because we all need to carefully consider, what we do with our lives, brings joy, comfort, peace, but not pain and suffering. And so naturally, we do not go out there and purposely look for things that would destroy our lives, I am sure we look for things that we know are best for ourselves, but sometimes we do make bad choices, which in turn bring consequences to our lives for prolonged period, we don't like that.

Besides, when we make those bad choices, we do not think about the pain they'll bring to our lives now, and perhaps those choices may help us to discover new things of this life so that we can learn from them and never to repeat them again. And yet at the same time there are many other things in life that are naturally detrimental for our lives even though we may see them as enjoyable as they can be, they are still wrong for our wellbeing. Therefore, we need to avoid at all cost those things to protect ourselves from the hardship they may bring to us, if not in a fleeting time, but perhaps in a long time.

For example, warning signs are very important to our lives especially the beaches sign, they are not to be ignored. As a matter fact, when they are ignored great risks come to play, not only to the subject in question, but also other people's lives as well who are trying to rescue the one whose life is in danger. When it comes to things that potentially dangerous to our lives or our wellbeing, we need not to ignore the warnings, we better listen and comply, so that we can be truly safe. It is not a matter of choice as you would do when buying groceries such as bread, drinks, or food for yourself and your family, you do not want people to tell you the choice to make when you are buying that kind of stuff, but you would want them to warn you if danger is present, that is going to hurt you and your family, and the ones you love after consuming these products, wouldn't you? So, you do understand you are not allowed for example to substitute diesel fuel for a vehicle that runs with gas just because your choice is what you want it to be since the warning reads "Unleaded only". The obvious is going to be, because of your choice, chances are the engine will be damaged and you will need to replace it with a new one.

Imagine you do that because this is your vehicle, your choice. Let's say you buy a new engine and the same day you go out there and repeat the same scenario, you put diesel in your car instead of unleaded gas; what do you think is going to happen? Then after that you continue to repeat the same thing over, and over, again for the rest of your life. Can you imagine what it would be like, if you continue making choices like that? I am sure Mr. Bill Gates a billionaire wouldn't want to make choices like that with his money, even if he wanted to, because there is no advantage, or benefit in doing things like that.

Likewise, it is important to notice that it is not the reality of somebody to come to your life uninvited and begin to tell you what you should and should not do with your life, which is not the case. The reality here is, that we all need to understand for the betterment, or the preservation, or the normalcy, if you will of humanity, the warning signs are ways that pertain to our lives, to guide us in the right paths for safety, so that we can prevent pain and suffering in our lives. Just like having to practice homosexuality, and other forms of sexual pervasions are detrimental for one's life, that is the reason why the creator of our lives gives us signs and warnings against such things, so that we can be safe and protected from the consequences of those warnings when ignored, in imposing our will against them.

Therefore, no one can stand blameless and irreproachable when facing the judge when the day comes. It is not a matter of what you want, but it is totally up to Him because He alone has the right and authority over you and over everything else there is in this life. My encouragement to you my friend, if you are practicing homosexuality in whatever form there is whether by choice, by experience, or you just don't care you do whatever you want, you need to seek help, so that you can get rid of the grip of that abnormal lifestyle behavior that is ultimately destructive for your life and the society. Just like you won't ignore the sign that reads "Danger or High voltage" please do so, don't ignore the sign when it comes to homosexuality.

PORNOGRAPHY ANOTHER SEXUAL PERVASION:

What is pornography? Well, to the best that I can describe it, I believe pornography is any type of sexual behavior that is being put in display for the sole reason of entertaining self, or others, whether private, or public. It is a violation of the fundamental principle that unites <u>one man and one woman in marriage relationship</u>. Pornography has always been viewed as graphic, dramatic, and dangerous to society that in the past, it was not accepted as normal, and so it is now. The word pornography is difficult to define. Again, in the past it was used broadly to refer to sexually explicit words, or images. Today the meaning of the term has been narrowed somewhat to describe sexually explicit material that is considered offensive.[6] It was something then, even that among the most liberals in the society, were advocating banning it publicly to safeguard the society from its paws. Children back then and children of our day were and are still the primary targets of such vicious weapon to mess up and destroy their lives entirely. It is primarily addictive, devilish, and detrimental for humanity. It is like a contagious disease that ruins lives, that begins from an individual to family units, and eventually to the entire society, if it does not stop spreading.

Now a day pornography is widely spoken among the pews, not specifically to help stopping the spread of it, but particularly to invite it in the people's lives, especially into the lives of those who have heard about it, and not experienced it, whether by entertaining, or involving in it. Perhaps you may say I am not worried about the effect of pornography in my life because I do not watch videos and look at magazines that support the spread of it. Yeah! That may be true, but what may be also true, and you probably don't know it yet, because if you are involving in promiscuity by having sex every once and awhile, or maybe one time with multiple partners that is an indication that you are involved in pornography.

Sometimes you may find those who are adamant to such behavior, and yet they can't help and think about it all the time, their thought life is stink, they visualize very vividly the ambiance of being with someone and lusting after sexual pleasures. Even though the imagery of a pornographic picture may seem harmless, also a scene from a movie just by looking at them, but the residual effect of that image can be far greater deadly.

Now, what makes pornography wrong? First, it is wrong because the master says so. Second, it is wrong because it is not up to us to decide what is right and what is wrong, for the fact we are not the author of life; we do not have a say in it. For this cause alone, we ought to pay attention to the things that we bring in our lives, which have great repercussion when acquire them, are contrary to the principle of life given by the creator. By the way, I mention the creator because in context of the creation and in relationship with an object to its maker. It is important to understand that we as human beings, we do have a boss so to speak who is in our lives, not to disturb us, but to encourage us in doing what's right always regardless the situation at hand. Not only that, since He created us, He also owned us, therefore, He wants the best for us, that is why He lays out ground rules to shape our lives while living on the earth to be the best we can, so that we wouldn't waste our life in vain pleasures of this world with no benefit such as pornography.

Now can pornography produce a pure and healthy life? Or would you use pornography as a teaching tool to be a good model citizen? So, if you can honestly answer without any uncertainty yes for these two questions, when obviously morally we cannot encourage this kind of life not only for the adults but much more exponentially no for the children because the damage by far is too much to contain. Now, let me draw your attention on something that I hope would be a major help to you in dealing with the subject of "pornography". The authority, upon which I build my case to speak so boldly against sexual perversion, does not come from man neither myself, nor any type of institution established such as school, church, or government for that matter, but it does come from a lone source that is the creator Himself. He is the one that created everything, which means He is sovereign over His creation, He has the right over everything He created including us mankind, to Him alone all due respect.

Friend understand this, when it comes to matter of authority, it does not matter what you really think or not, it is simply a matter of submission. I would agree with you, it depends to whom you submit to, because submission is straightly a matter of the heart, and it also comes with a price attached to it, for the fact that it allows us to demonstrate where we pledge allegiance to. Either we pledge allegiance to the one that has all power, the one that created you and me, the one that knows everything there is to know in life, the one that has power over life and death; or either we can pledge allegiance to a man that literally possesses nothing only perhaps wishful thinking ideas or ideology, who has no power, no control over nature. Or perhaps, we can pledge allegiance also to a form of institution established that has governmental strength, or military might, or technology capability to advance scientifically, to efficiently destroy more lives on the planet. So, which is it exactly your allegiance pledged to, since your choice matters for either the preservation of life, and for the destruction of it?

That is the reason why when we talk about the perversity of pornography in the sexual context, it is not about what we think, for my friend we can think all we want about it, debating what is wrong or what is right about it, but until He say what He thinks, none of our debating and selfish ideas would matter much, because He is the one that has the final say. He is the creator therefore, He is the boss, and that He is forever to whom our allegiance ought to be, for preserving our lives while we adhere to His principles that protect us against the stains of devilish immoral proportion insanity such as homosexuality, lesbianism, bestiality, pornography, transvestite, prostitution, promiscuity, pimpism, fornication, extramarital affair, adultery and other more sexual perversions that exist.

Our creator by the way is a loving creator, He makes sure that we are indeed safe physically, morally, emotionally, educationally, and spiritually, because these ingredients are in fact components of a healthy wellbeing person. We do not want to deviate from the fact that we have a loving master that is looking out for our welfare and interest in life. If only we understand His heart toward us all, we would not have acted the way we did so far, from the beginning of this world. We would be satisfied and would have the pleasure of a lifetime that we would not trade for anything less of this world, which brought us pain and suffering all along the way. It is my sincere belief that we can turn the table around before it is too late, if only we decide to seek for His guidance and connect with Him truly base on the knowledge that He has, the ultimate power to keep us safe throughout our lifetime no matter the condition life turns to be for us. So, it is not about us, but it is about all He wants, we need to get a grip of ourselves to get rid of pornography, homosexuality, lesbianism activities or other sexual perversions for His sake, which would benefit us greatly because of what He has done for in Sodom and Gomorrah He can still do, be careful and pay Attention!

ANOTHER SEXUAL PERVERSION "MASTURBATION"

Many of whom have gotten involved in deeply great sexual perversion are the ones who most likely debuted at the earliest age of their lives with masturbation. Such behavior has been chronic in their lives secretly that for several reasons have used their body in numerous occasions to, so call satisfy their sexual desires, to reduce the intensity of the sexual drive, which keeps them on edge to want even more. Let it be known unto you now and forever more that masturbation is a lost not a gain. It in fact affects the whole person, the mind, the spirit, the body and the soul. It does not really bring pleasure, as a matter of fact, if there is anything that it gives, it is only regret, guilt, and shame, because after wasting time being alone with yourself, you'll notice immediately that your sense of worth is gone. It would seem as if you've been reduced to a piece of nothingness, and even though there is nobody around, you feel so embarrassed and that the thought of suicide comes right into your mind to somehow alleviate the pain as the guilt rushing through your spirit.

Masturbation can be very dangerous and perhaps deadly, because not only it weights so much on your spirit, but also it can drain the body tremendously at the level of passing out and physical exhaustion mercilessly. As you are continually engaged in such activity, it will in effect become a strong hold in your life, which is truly a violation against the nature of sexual satisfaction. Even though it may seem to deliberate you both from having to involve with someone prematurely sexually, and from the thought of your immediate sexual need to be met, but the residual effect of such act can cause you to be violent, arrogant, impatient, insane, and easily to lose temper.

Consequently, your involvement in such a way to acquire self satisfaction, it can lead you to deeply seek comfort in watching pornographic material, and it will give you a distorted view of the opposite sex where it will simply be a means to an end for sexual fulfillment, not to be regarded as to have a normal, or to nurture a healthy relationship. When you look at masturbation, or self-gratification as we know it of, it seems to mean another way of fulfilling your sexual desire, but in fact, it is another way to say that I can do it all alone, I don't need anybody else to be part of my life I am self-sufficient, no! Thank you I don't need your help. It is a selfish expression from one to avoid at all cost relationship with another person of the opposite sex which is perfectly normal, if engaging in the proper context by the way.

From the beginning when the male man was given the female, it was intended for them to have a wonderful relationship with each other in every aspect of their lives, and most of all to have sexual relationship, because it was for them to enjoy each other more, also it was for the continual procreation. And so, when an individual most likely a man is involving in masturbating himself to find sexual satisfaction, he is basically throwing substance that is in effect vital for the work of pro-creation. When he delivers the product in the ground *(if you know what I mean)* he is constantly wasting not only his energy, but seriously the very fabric of mankind by which he is responsible to bring others into this world, which also begins through a relationship with the opposite sex.

What a waste! for some of you, you may think it is alright for anybody to find sexual pleasure however he/she sees fit to do so, it is not anybody's business, nobody needs to follow anybody's rules regarding this. It is up to the person himself, not a mother or dad, or friends, or any form of authority for that matter. It is only a private matter to deal with in a discrete conceivable way. Yes, indeed it is a private matter, no one should come in between to discuss anybody's life to try fixing it; it is totally abnormal, why? Because you and I were not created to seek to satisfy ourselves sexually in this condition. We were created to be involved in series of relationships whether it'd be familial relationship, mom, dad, brother sister, or friendship relationship, work relationship, and romantic relationship, where there is marriage, sexual intimacy, and in turn to repeat the same cycle as to where you came from, which also lead to where you started your own family. Because of that, we are creatures of relationship, we cannot live with ourselves to be considered as relationship, therefore we must pursue others in making friends which will turn to dating, which will turn to engagement which turns to be marriage relationship with each other, while we respect the principles and the norms established for each relationship distinctively, without violating the core values of each one of them among ourselves human beings.

Incidentally, I have been a victim of such activity for many years. I did not think when I first started that this could have a tremendous effect upon my life, not only for trying to keep it a secret, but also my perception in life in relationship with opposite sex to think of me less of a person, that I would not be able to make them aware of my sexual need, that I would rather take care of it on my own. Besides, I also knew then, that I had to openly express my longing desires in this area of my life. I would have to violate the principle that only in marriage relationship one can be sexually active. For this reason, I had to find a way to dismiss the idea of having sexual relationship with a woman that I was not married to. I thought that the fact I had two wrong viable options to choose from, so I chose each time I was confronted with the same dilemma the lesser evil of the two which was "Masturbation".

Was it the only way out to come to safety? Perhaps at the time it was for me the only way I could escape from being trap within myself as I was burning in flame with sexual desires to avoid being involved with a woman, which might have dire consequences to follow such as venereal diseases, pregnancy, and to protect my testimony with fear that my name would not associate with someone that my parents, or friends would not approve of.

It was later in my life after I had a wonderful encounter with my creator that I discovered that I was here for a purpose to live for Him in a way even though not married yet at the time, I still had sexual desires, that I was longing for companionship that I could still go through life with self-control over my desires whatever they may be physical, or emotional without interrupting the grace He has given me to put down this stronghold in my life. I can tell you, even though after many years of marriage, that the temptation has come in many occasions, but by His grace I don't have to be a victim anymore, I am more than a conqueror over this temptation. I am sure that there may be others like me out there whose battles have not been easy, because they are facing a giant that is bigger than their effort, bigger than their ideas, or the power they have even though they may also have everything they need at their disposal to fight, they still losing the fight.

Hang on, you are in a good place in your life right now, it shows you that you need help for your situation, it gives you perspective that whatever your life is worth, it is worth more with the help of the one who has created you. If your problem is masturbation just like it was mine, you don't need to be a victim anymore, you simply need to put away your own desire to accept His purpose for your life in considering obeying His word and follow His righteousness, you will be a conqueror even over masturbation by His grace.

The most advanced, unfortunately, money making machineries are "people". However, money can never be made by none other than people, for it is good for them in any society for distinct reasons, and various needs. Therefore, the question that comes in mind, can we live without it? I believe it is safe to say that because of our current state of living, our dependence on energy, infrastructure, medicine, technology, schools, government, food, and so forth we human beings cannot live without money for the most part because of its significance in our lives.

It has been made fact that millions upon millions of dollars are being invested worldwide in various markets out there in search of great profit revenues, so that the people of the world can be mostly financially sound in maintaining a rewarding modality of life in joy and happiness.

Ever since man left the position of lack for anything, the garden of Eden that is, the directives that were given to him by God "cursed is the ground for thy sake, in sorrow shalt thou eat of it all the days of thy life… in the sweat of thy face shalt thou eat bread till thou return unto the ground." (**Gen. 3:17, 19**) have propelled him to work even harder with an ambitious agenda to be rich in wanting nothing.[7] Because of man's heart's condition, he has become human machinery to accomplish such agenda no matter the condition may be to attain his goal. Therefore, to be without money, it is not an option, he will do whatever it takes, he may to acquire it, for it is the only reason he lives for. Such things as immorality, sin is not going to be hindrances to keep him from reaching his goals, and perhaps it may well be that he will use these sinful things in nature to his advantage, to accumulate wealth beyond measure.

To begin working toward his goal, one of the areas that he would tackle to get what he wants first, after he made a good assessment, is the human trafficking. Since you know as well as I do that there are many categories of people living on the earth such as: there are the have people, and there are the have not people. To be precise, the have are the ones we consider normally "the rich people" and the have not are "the poor people".

Needless to say, we know that there are people in some parts of the world that are barely able to survive hunger, let alone having a decent condition of living as oppose to many, where food, water, clothing, shelter, and all the necessities of life are not a concern. These have not people certainly, are no lesser people than the ones who do have, and do not struggle for survival. The difference here is the have ones may have been privileged to be blessed more with earthly goods than the have not ones, which they in turn may have been blessed in some other areas in life different from the have ones. The fact of the matter is, we will find ourselves in either one of these categories of life in learning to live with each other regarding, or regardless the category we fall under.

Unfortunately, there is always going to be the have ones and the have not around, that's the nature of life, and sometimes we also find that there are some that would transpose from one side to the other vice a versa because of circumstances of life they have to go through for better, or for worse. The ones, that have more they can ever imagine, are working so hard to continue maintaining a standard of life to always have, and at the same time the ones, who do not have, are continuing to work hard to see themselves one day out of misery, out of the financial struggle of life, to taste a bit the joy of living, where this weight of life and suffering can be at last gone, or vanished away for good.

You know in the early days of the first century, it was allowed that rich individuals could buy, sell, and own a person known as "slave, or servant" in order to bring about economical stability, the right to trade and exchange goods, so that life could have a sense of worth and meaningful social relationship that helped develop ways for global economic growth. Unfortunately, sacrifices had to be made through the means of human trafficking, because it was solely the fastest way for economic growth among nations since industrialization was at its birth for instance: the construction of maritime ships for commerce worldwide, and the building of iron roads for locomotive transportations, and as well as ports for harboring ships upon arrivals. Since then, man always looking out to find the next thing to do to attain, which is by the way, the same old goal, which is to accumulate wealth regardless how he gets it, is not an issue, and perhaps his strategy to acquire wealth may cause him to do the most immoral thing, whereas he would rationalize it to the benefit of his pocket no matter is the cost.

In the back of his mind, he understood early that power is nice to have, and for him the fastest way to have it is to accumulate a great deal of wealth, meaning to be powerful, you must have money, which also means you have power. In progressing from the realm of human trafficking from one continent to another, there has been development of crude human sexual behaviors among the slaves and as well as the slave traders. It happened all the time through the voyages at sea, the slave masters would not disregard the opportunity to profit lucratively from clients who embarked their ships who might solicit sexual favors with the slaves from their masters regardless ages, gender, or sizes, because it opened an all new way of money making.

Therefore, it became accustomed to human trafficking that people, especially women the young ones, were being mistreated, abused, violated their rights, because they were not considered as human beings, but a means to an end, if they did what they were bought for. It was not regarded these type of abuses as being unlawful, for the fact that slaves did not have rights, not only that, but also, they, as slaves, saw themselves as such just to avoid their chances of survival, if ever they were to be bought for domestic services, they knew they would be better off, only if they did what they were told.

Furthermore, it was commonly accepted that the followings were the categories of people: the noble, the clergy, and the mass. Ordinarily the majority the world's population would fall under the mass' category, because before there was civilization most of the lands of the world were called colonies, since they were occupied by the kings and the queens of the world, or the nobles. So, it was not an element of surprise to know that anybody who was not from the category of the noble was automatically a slave because by default he/she was a slave to the king, or the queen, they owned it all, even though there has not been a chain that locked the feet and hands, the understanding was, everybody was the king's period. There is this saying during the time of the colony that says I am paraphrasing "Everything comes and goes for the metropolis". The idea behind this saying was to remind the mass that anything that belongs to them also belongs to the king without exception, even their children as well.

The mindset of the society today is no different from back then, where the system of exploitation is continuing to ravage the weak, the vulnerable, whether forcefully, or voluntarily, given them into the mix because of economic hardship. For this reason, it has been rather desperate for many of those, who are impatiently looking for a life of grandeur with no expense restrictions, under the umbrella of capitalism, have engaged themselves in various illicit activities such as: human trafficking, sex trafficking, slavery, prostitution, and others.

Throughout the world we find countless of people that connect to do just that, to gain control and create what I call **"Economic discrimination".** Economic discrimination, it is in search for freedom and independence from want, whereby buying and spending can be done without adding more pain or suffering, but rather with pleasure, to intentionally meet the present needs for the sake of wellbeing. This is for this reason, for the most part, that immorality seems to be prevailing in a society, where the average person is struggled ten times more than two generations ago for these basic needs of life. They are shelter, food, and clothing.

Imagine what one would do when there is no food on the table, or perhaps when there is no place to stay to be called home.

It would be as easy as to drink a cup of water to fall into immorality when those needs are overwhelmingly present day in and day out with no glimpse of hope, that there will be a better tomorrow. When one has already exhausted all resources to keep up with the normalcy of life, what is left to do? It is not too difficult to turn from righteousness to unrighteousness since misery is not sweet, it destroys lives, families, people, and nations, because of its venomous taste it gives to those whose lives have been touched by it. Those who are affected as such continue to wonder and question the author of life why He allows so many to go with such great needs in their lives, and so many others to have so much. As they look at life from this perspective, they can see this economic discrimination, which they are so upset about, and that there is not much they can do to change it, except to find a way legally, or illegally to bypass it, and find themselves in the other side of it.

The ideal solution response to such a critical matter of one's life is, to go out looking for a job, which in turn will help alleviate the pain of hunger at least in a brief time, but in long time the goal is to eliminate the three distinct basic needs in life to be safe totally. When really, it is impossible to even scratch the surface of one's basic needs of everyday to survive, it becomes evident, that something of a drastic measure is about to happen.

The critical point of decision making to bring about relief, or workable solution to resolve the problem, will filter without a doubt through that individual state of character, his moral compass, to determine where to position him/herself to acquire help for the next day's meal. By the way, I use the verb "To position" here very carefully to mean in the manner of association, in other word as you're looking for help, you're going to associate yourself with other people that perhaps went through the same situation as you, or others that can make things happen even though they may not have gone through comparable situation. You may find myriad of people, or places to go to for help, which will result to dire consequences with great financial gain, or also you may only have one shot at success, where the result can be, if things go wrong, either jail, or lying in a casket ready to be buried.

Remember, anything that anybody undertakes to do is always a reflection of his character. It is to say, once a person comes to this one fork of his life, he's got some serious thinking to do, in applying wisdom to show the very best of his character, because of his decision.

When the very basic needs of life are not met daily in someone's life, he will make a turn to seek for help, and the help he would find would either change his life in an effective way, or in a worse conceivable way than ever before his previous way of life. Some in this lifetime whose lives have been tremendously crippled by economic hardship, where the necessities of life basically are not met, would turn to drugs, alcohol, prostitution, gambling, and other kinds of immorality to find both relief and comfort about their problems. Some because of hopelessness, and the intensity of their pain, while fighting both the giant problem of being unable to provide for themselves, and to keep their sanity intact, have contemplated suicidal thoughts, where they've come to the end of themselves with such irrational selfish idea that life is not worth living in that condition.

I have been reminded, of my own father ordeal long ago before I was even born, by my grandfather that he was about to take his own life on two separate occasions, while he was a young man, having in him great hopes and dreams. Understand this, my father was a very sensitive and reserved type of person all his life, he would not talk about his problems, his worries, his failures, not even his successes in life. He was more of a person that would put his life on the line for others just to make it easy for them, but as a young man about the age of twenty-five, perhaps younger, he would find himself at a crossroad to the point he would without a doubt end his life, because he was unable to meet his basic needs, and his future was certainly unsure. Imagine for him after losing his mother in his early age, and his father was not around most of the time to provide for him, where he found it necessary to care for himself very early in life which caused him to be overwhelmed and fatigued, to know that he had to take up responsibility as a man with no preparation and experiences to do so.

It was just about when he had finished tying the knot from the rope he would use to hang himself on a tree, which by the way was very common those days, that my grandfather was coming from a habitual path that he would usually take after taking care of his cattle and lands that he had in the neighborhood, since he was a farmer by trade, he saw the man who would eventually be my father there with a looped rope in his hand hanging from the tree next to him. Suddenly he approached him and said "What in the world you think you're doing? Is there anything else to do, God forbid?" Rapidly he intercepted the rope from my father's hands, and from there he took him under his wings, and he became his mentor, a father figure for him. Later as he was one of my grandfather's hired men living in his house, he would become his son-in-law, for he had married my mother, my grandfather's second child, his first daughter.

So, you see my father would have died, if he had not been rescued by my grandfather just because of the fact, as a young man he would not accept to continue living his life, not having somehow a definitive concrete plan for his life, with a glimpse of hope of a sure future. The reality is, that it is not certain on a step by step stand point what life would be like in the future, but at least it calms the spirit to know that the basic needs are being met at this level daily, which put away the worries of today, in working with sure hope toward a bright tomorrow.

Now with that in mind, it does not mean that anybody who's ever been involved in any type of immorality in the past or will be involved in such a thing in the future, would do it because of poverty, or because of being unable to provide for their basic needs of life. No, no, no, it is because of the person's state of character, his world view of life in general reflects his decision making, where lacking things can be evidence of the heart toward morality no matter the circumstance in life may be. At the same time, we do not want to ignore that there are many who would not hesitate to take the easy road of immorality should the opportunity present itself before them. We do not want to judge anybody in particular because of the choices they make, in thinking because we do not do, or embrace their paths in life that we must be better than they are.

Not at all, as the matter fact, we are just like they are, the only difference for those of us who choose morality in life is, we make our decision not based on our circumstances in life, but rather in accordance with the fundamental principles of life given by God Almighty when it comes to right and wrong. Therefore, those who are not in compliance with the God's fundamental principles of life would suffer greatly, beginning with the basic needs of life, because these things are in effect consequential of a heart that entertains immorality, even if it is not practiced openly.

What about those who greatly benefit for being involved in sinful acts, and immoral and sexual perversion such as; pornography, homosexuality, lesbianism, prostitution, adultery, fornication, bestiality, and others? There is an old saying that says "Put on a beat on the dog, but you can rest assured wait for his master" which means in perspective of this particular subject we are dealing with, that no one will go unpunished after committed sin.[9] Sin like prostitution, homosexuality, adultery, and so forth, it is a direct violation of God's principles regarding sexual relationship, and it is in fact an abomination before Him, for He cannot and will not tolerate this type of behavior, he will punish the sin and the sinner because He is holy.

Friend don't be surprised to know that there are others like us that devote themselves to bring about morality and decency among humanity, so that we can comply with the norms and God's principles regarding sexual activities. Among those people we have (CWA) Concerned Women for America who is standing in the gap to alert both the people of God and those who are wandering out

WHY GUILT . . . . AFTER SEX

there without God and no hope in the world. A few years back, they posted an article on their websites entitled "Pornography and Figures" which dated August 10, 2010 by Janet M. Larue. In this article we find out the staggering enormous figures of revenues made by those who are currently involved in the porn business whether directly, or indirectly.[10]

For examples, we have revenue for adult videos was $20 billion; for sex clubs $5 billion; magazines $7.5 billion; phone sex $4.5 billion; escort services $11 billion; cable/ satellite/ pay-per view-TV $2.5 billion; CD-ROMs/DVD-ROMs $1.5 billion; internet sales and memberships $1.5 billion; novelties $1 billion; and others $1.5 billion. These figures are currently for the most part the thrust of the American economy regardless the nature of the business even though they are immoral, but they are greatly appreciated, because their contribution to the economy helps support the American people nonetheless. Should this be an excuse to allow the prevalence of sinful behavior, or immorality in our midst? Not at all, I think we are supposed to radically as human beings eradicate all type of nuisances that threaten our lives both physically and emotionally, so that we would not have to worry about incurable diseases entrapment, which would hinder us to fulfill God's given destiny for our lives. This notion of economic growth, or perhaps the fight against the economic discrimination should not be a means by which we validate our sinful behavior both privately and publically. It ought to be a shame and a prideful motivation to be in the offense against such sinful behavior to be better off, because God said "Better is little with the fear of the Lord than great treasure and trouble therewith" **Prov. 15:16**.[11] Another one God said "Better is a little with righteousness than great revenues without right" **Prov.16:8**.[12] I believe the ideal position we all should have is, the one that is truly secured and anchored in the word of God, rather than in our own wisdom, or the word of man, or in the sinful behavior that can bring financial gain for that matter.

The article goes on to say that "porn revenue is bigger than all combined revenues of all the professional football, baseball, and basketball franchises".[13] It is a fact that a nation is stronger both economically and militarily when practiced righteousness according to God's word "Righteousness exalteth a nation, but sin is a reproach to any people" **Prov.14:34**.[14] If practicing immorality, or sinful behaviors are American ways because of freedom and liberty to do so: may these American ways be condemned, I will still follow God's way.

If involving in any sexual impurity such as homosexuality, lesbianism, adultery, and so forth are American ways for financial gain, may they all be condemned, I will still choose God's way because it is great to position yourself with God's way, meaning to associate yourself with Him to really experience freedom, security both physically and emotionally, and to truly benefit financially since He owns it all. He said in His word that "... godliness with contentment is great gain. For we brought nothing into this world, and it is certain that we can carry nothing out. And having food and raiment let us be therewith content; but they that will be rich fall into temptation and a snare, and into many foolish and hurtful lusts which drown men in destruction and perdition. For the <u>love of money</u> is the root of all evil which while some coveted after, they have erred from the faith, and pierced themselves through many sorrows" **I Tim.6:6-10**.[15]

Not only that God owns it all, it is something that we all need to keep in perspective every single day of our lives, especially those who are His children, because this truth applies in connection with His creation, for He has created it all for His glory as revealed in the image of His dear Son Jesus Christ **Col.1:15-19** "Who is the image of the invisible God (Jesus) the first born of every creature, for by Him were all things created, that are in heaven, and that are in earth, visible and invisible, whether they be thrones, or dominions, or principalities, or powers all things were created by Him, and for Him. And He is before all things, and by Him all things consist, and He is the head of the body, the church; that is the beginning, the first born from the dead that in all things He might have the preeminence, for it pleased the Father that in Him should all fullness dwell".[16]

This quoting of the scriptures is not a desperate attempt to bring you to Christ, although it might be necessary for many, but it is instead a way to state the facts about the reality of our existence into this planet earth, in an effort for all to truly recognize the one who has created it all, so that no matter what our perspective may be on things regarding the world and everything in it to make an argument, would not stand a chance before Him. For God made it all, He made it all possible for all of us to rejoice, to have fun during all the days of our lives here on earth, he did not ask from us anything in return, He simply gave it all even the best He had He gave on the cross of Calvary, His Son Jesus was crucified as a sacrifice to demonstrate His great love for mankind while we still reject Him (**Romans 5:8).**

Keep in mind, when we came into this world at birth, we did not bring anything along, the moment we opened our eyes for the first time, there it was everything in place waiting for us, even though we could not comprehend it all from our little mind then, we were still able to have the privilege to use the things of His creation such as: the air, the sun, the heat, the cold, food, water, day and night so forth. Now because of our physiology development, in other words, we grow older, we think we can take over this planet earth, we think we can outsmart God whom has created it all, to think that we can tell Him that He has no right over His creation. Who do we think we are? Listen to what He has to say about our life "For what is your life? It is even a vapor that appeareth for a little time, and then vanisheth away" **James 4:14.**[17] So you can see my friend, don't sweat it, we cannot and should not stand in opposition with God, for He sees our life as a vapor before Him and the rest is history. Don't even try to puff up yourself, you are nothing before Him at all, we are temporal, He is eternal, be careful!

Now, considering the revealing nature of God Almighty and

His character, from what we read in His words, how come we've drifted so far away for His obvious plan for our lives, where we manufacture our lives both privately and publicly to be purposely sinful especially in sexual activities? God says, in His word that "For this is the will of God even your sanctification, that you abstain from fornication, that every one of you should know how to possess his vessel in sanctification and honor not in the lust of concupiscence even as the gentiles which know not God ... for God hath not called us unto uncleanness, but unto holiness" **I Thes.4:3-5, 7**. Yes indeed! The reality of this passage is for a specific group of people, God's children, but however the application of it is also true and important that every single person on the planet of this earth is called unto righteousness, precisely to abstain to any kinds of sexual perversion before God. Make no mistake about that friend! God will always judge the sin and as well as the sinner.[18,]

You've noticed that I shared with you a little bit of my father's life as he had been under a great deal of pressure, which he had considered to end his life. Surely enough in a sort of odd, or mysterious way his life was spared by my grandfather, which allowed him to position himself to receive help and assistance from my grandfather who gave him opportunity of a second chance in life to pursue his goals and ambition, which later he would become one of the most respectable persons in the community. The only problem was, for him and so it would for everybody else, that he had to make his choice to determine his destination in focusing on his circumstances to find freedom.

For him, it has been somewhat obscure as to what he would want to be later in life since first, he did not have a formal education upon which he could have had a career to be proud of, but unfortunately, that's what he had to fight so hard, unlike others to save himself from poverty and other difficulties in life that were constantly in the way. Second, because struggles were part of his daily life, he was convinced that he was inferior among others that he had to prove himself worthy of a person, and most of all worthy of a man, even though he was not seen as inferior by his friends and family, but accepted it as such, so that he could fight his giants head on. Thirdly and finally, he knew that he has been an extra load in my grandfather's home, he needed to move out to cover back his shame as he would venture to take a leap of faith, in pursuing a romantic relationship with my grandfather's first daughter.

Needless to say, to be able to become my grandfather's son-in-law is considered to be a great deal of success regarding his low self-esteem to make it thus far was surreal. After many years had gone, and after marrying my mother, my father had become one of the richest men in the village. He had lands, cattle, houses, cars, and other things, and hired servants, and certainly money that one would say he made it. The question is how did he make it? Or what did he do that changed his life in a positive way?

CHAPTER 5

THE BEAUTY OF SEX

In retrospect, where did the idea of sexual relation come from? Who started it? And by what authority were they able to engage as such? Did they break any law in engaging themselves that way and many other times after that? Perhaps I am sure there are many questions that you would love to get answered regarding this topic. Unfortunately, we won't be able to pose and answer all of them at this time, but I will, and assure you as we are going through these series of answers together, you will be able to have a better understanding, in attempting to clarify some of the obscures of sexual relation avenues, and at the same time unveiling the true beauty of sex in its proper context as it relates to men and women.

Remember, as I mentioned before, that men and women are creatures of relationship. We human beings cannot survive life itself without relationship at any level, because the fact of the matter is, the very fabric of our being as human begins with relationship, in other words, we are all the product of two people of the opposite sexes in combination to reproduce the very you in existence, which in turn you will do to bring forth kids in relationship with another person of the opposite sex.

As you can see, relationship is very important to human beings regardless your social status. A medical doctor needs a mechanic to fix his car when it breaks down; the same a mechanic needs a doctor to examine his heart problem vice a versa. Just like a chef needs a farmer to cultivate his crops that allows the chef to cook for people, the same a musician needs an instrument maker to fashion instruments, so that musicians such as him will be able to perform and produce great music for the enjoyment and the entertainment of great music lovers. The same also we all need law enforcement officers to serve and protect us from criminals out there as they do need us to help them solve difficult cases as well.

With that in mind, apart from the greatest relationship an individual has the privilege to have with his creator, <u>sexual relation</u> is the most vitally, crucially important relationship that a man can have with a woman vice a versa, because first, it is not a relationship that is simply physical, but at the very core of it is spiritual, for the fact it has been given to us, and ordained by God. Secondly, it is a different kind of relationship unlike others where two people of opposite sexes can actually, and literally become one, which has eternal consequences both good and evil. In perspective, human relationships naturally both man and woman gear toward that kind of relationship automatically, so that the fulfilling process of God's intention for mankind in relationship with Him will bring forth His revealing nature to us "His love".

At this time, let me introduce to you the very word of God Almighty if I may, that we missed wholly and consequently brought us pain, disorder, disagreement, problems, and death. God said: **"IT IS NOT GOOD THAT THE MAN SHOULD BE ALONE, I WILL MAKE HIM AN HELP MEET FOR HIM" Gen.2:18.**[1] From there because of these words that God had said "IT **IS NOT GOOD THAT THE MAN SHOULD BE ALONE**" the Lord God established "**relationship**" not only that, but the obvious was very clear to Adam in contrast with the animal beings after naming them all one by one, and that he did not have an help meet. Therefore, God said: "I **WILL MAKE HIM AN HELP MEET FOR HIM**" since "FOR **ADAM THERE WAS NOT FOUND AN HELP MEET FOR HIM**" Gen.2:20.[2]

Because God knew how important relationship was among the animal beings for their survival, the same He wanted it for human beings in general as well as companionship. So you see friend, this was the very first time that God said these words " It is not good" since everything He has done as far as creation concerned, He would always say that it <u>was very good</u>, but when it came to Adam being alone, God saw there was no good in that so, from there He was going to fix the problem right away at the moment for the male man Adam, and at the same time would set precedence for generations to follow that, it has been ordained by Him for men and women to never be alone physically in term of relationship.

In the context of heterosexual relationship, God administered the very first anesthesia if you will to Adam by causing him to fall into a deep sleep (**Gen.2:21**) which He would pull from Adam's side a rib, a rib that would become a significant part of Adam's life after that as He would present to him another person of the same kind such as Adam of a different gender (female) .[3] Adam would call her name "Eve" because she was drawn from him as he said "This is now the bone of my bones, and flesh of my flesh" **Gen.2:23**, and she was also called the mother of all living (**Gen.3:20**).[4]

Friend while you are following the progression that is taking place as God is orchestrating ways to fulfill His plan in the life of the first man "Adam". Keep in mind, that God explicitly made it for Adam to see that he was indeed alone and that it was perfectly normal for him to want someone to relate with, while he was in the place where God had put him in the Garden of Eden. God purposely demonstrated to Adam that his physical need was of utmost importance for both Adam and Himself, because later He would command Adam to be fruitful and multiply the earth (**Gen.1:28**).[5] Therefore when He (God) would bring "Eve" to Adam, it was to complete Adam as a person within himself, but at the same time God did not want to create another person with a mass of dust again from the ground just like He did with Adam, instead He drew "Eve" from Adam which He has already created, which also symbolized the process by which everyone would come into being such as to reproduce after their kind, even did the animal beings that God commanded (**Gen.1**).[6]

God did not draw from Adam's side a rib to bring into being another person, although of the same kind, not the same gender as he to bring her to Adam, so that they can have a relationship. That was not the precedence that God had given to us human being, but instead after He brought "Eve" to Adam He said the followings: "Therefore shall a man (male) leave his father and his mother, and shall cleave unto his wife (female) : and they shall be one flesh" **Gen.2:24**.[7] From this snapshot of history, you have been both seen enfold the principle by which God intended for two people of opposite sexes to come together as one, meaning sexually engaged, and witnessed the very first wedding ceremony of the very first two people God created. A wedding ceremony that was performed by God Almighty Himself, whence there He instituted family, the institution by which He placed to uphold His standards as mirrors to reflect His will on earth as it is in heaven, according to His word (**Matt.6:10**).[8]

Now Adam and Eve, they both were new at engaging themselves as such sexually, simply because there was not anybody else before them who have done that which they could have learned it from, neither could they have learned it from their moms and dads since they were not products of human reproduction, instead they were created by God Himself with His own hands. So far, God was pleased with His creation, as well as His first two opposite sexes that have come together as one, under the umbrella of God's protection of sexual engagement.

If you notice, that there was not anything embarrassing between the two of them at this time, right after they have been pronounced husband and wife by God. The assumption here that fundamentally husbands and wives are come together sexually for the first time in their lifetime with no fear of sexual violation, which was exactly what they needed to do to seal this covenant, not only among themselves, but also with God until death due them apart.

This covenant is a blood covenant, because with their first sexual contact initially anticipates <u>the shedding of the blood</u> which marks the authenticity of such covenant guaranteed a lifetime, which also symbolizes indeed that this relationship is of God and for God (**Gen.15:7-21**).[9] This coming together of two people of the opposite sexes as one is one of the ways we can experience the beauty of sex, for the fact first of all, this is the place it should happen legally, and second of all, it guarantees a lifetime covenant before God between two lives protected by Him, in order to carry out His plan throughout their lifetime.

Besides, when God asks a man to leave his father and his mother to cleave unto his wife, according to **Genesis 2:24**, He initially calls upon that man to a life of service, to commit himself in bringing about God's plan in the family, that He entrusts him with. He is going to love, provide, protect his wife, and to live with her according to knowledge, to honour her as unto the weaker vessel (**1 Peter3:1-7; Eph. 5:21-33; Col.3:18-19**) to bring up his children in the nurture and the admonition of the Lord (**Eph.6:4**) and to train them in the way they should go (**Prov. 22:6**) and to teach them the commandments of the Lord (**Deut. 6:1-10**).[10]

And so, his wife will come along side as an help meet to complete her husband, to put in action God's plan according to her husband's calling. She needs to show reverence to her husband, knowing that he is the head of the house, and that it is him that God calls to lead just like God did with Christ for the church (**Eph. 5:21-33**).[11] So it is through the sexual relation within the parameter of marriage that God can and will fulfill His plan among humanity to please Himself, and so that we in turn can enjoy life fully, and live happily ever after as you may say.

Furthermore, notice **Genesis 2:25.** It says that "they were both naked, the man and his wife, and were not ashamed".[12] First, in context we do know that they were literally naked which they had to sew fig leaves together for themselves, and so did God with coats of skins for covering (**Gen.3:7; 3:21**), but at the same time their nakedness put them in the right context of husbands and wives should be to enjoy sexual pleasure as married couples. They did not notice that they were naked before even though they were until God had brought them together, just to initiate their relationship upon the foundation of being <u>one flesh,</u> according to God's word (**Gen.2:24**).[13] Also, if you look at right in the middle part of the 25th verse it says; "the man and his wife" it does not say the man and the woman like it says in the 22th verse "And the rib which the Lord God had taken from man, made He a woman, and brought her unto the man". The language here has changed in the context of marriage relationship because the word "wife" of verse 25 deals with the idea that Eve was not simply a woman, but she was also the wife of Adam which entails that they have the right to be sexually engaged based on the prerogative of God's word found in verse 24 the word "cleave".[14]

Therefore, they were not under any violation, and that is why they were not ashamed according to the latter part of the 25th verse, because in the context of marriage relationship first of all, they should not be, and second of all, because that is what God wanted them to do to carry out His mandate that He gave them according to **Genesis 1:28** "God said unto them, be fruitful, and multiply, and replenish the earth, and subdue it ..." I am sure you and I cannot help and notice, that the only way that they could be fruitful and multiply, and replenish the earth, and subdue it, was only through sexual relation within the boundaries of marriage relationship of course, and so it is for us today to do our part in replenishing the earth, and being fruitful, and multiplying, is only as it was then through sexual relation within the bonds of marriage. That is again another way of the beauty of sex.[15]

Look friend, the beauty of sex is not on the level of performance of an individual, whether in or outside the bonds of marriage, when being sexually engaged, nor is it because an individual regularly active as to how it is almost impossible for him/her not to do it, because that's the only reason he/she lives for; or money can be

WHY GUILT . . . . AFTER SEX

made, lots of them in such a way it becomes relatively speaking to the beauty of sex since the profit drawn from such activity is totally satisfying. But at the same time, as we look at the damages that occurred over the years, and still are happening in our days as the results of wrong kinds of sexual activities; can we really see the beauty of sex? Such activities like being promiscuous, involving with multiple partners sexually at once, exposing oneself in front of a camera to pose for pornographic magazines, or perhaps performing oneself for pornographic videos with stuff that can endanger one's life in doing it, with also both people and animals for enjoyment and entertainment, or perhaps perverting oneself by being involved in homosexuality to satisfy one's lustful desires.

The beauty of sex is not also practicing the so called "safe sex" when a man, or a woman manages to come out a relationship with lots of sexual activities involved with no strings attached such as: kids, no bills to pay, and as well as no commitment, and no promise of marriage, where somehow the use of condoms, or some other type of preservative materials have been used to prevent both pregnancies, and sexual transmitted diseases (STD). As the matter of fact, the so called (safe sex) according to the world's standard is anything but safe, just for the fact, the very same things that are being used to bring protection from venereal diseases, or to give meaningful sexual pleasures, are also the very things that put one's life in jeopardy and in violation with the fundamental principles of sexual engagement.

The so called "safe sex" is focusing more on the idea of how to prevent passing on sexual transmitted diseases, and yet at the same time, is building a platform for sexual debauchery where the emotional and the spiritual impact are neglected all along. From a world stand point, the so called "safe sex" is not viewed as being right and wrong, it is simply accepted as a daily necessity of life, one that can be regarded as normal as having a regular meal every day to survive. It is in effect a phenomenon that occurs daily among the sexes without thinking twice about it, because the reality is to them; there is not a big deal about two people, or preferably two adults who are having sex if they agree upon it. They just need to make sure that they practice "safe sex", the use of condoms, or perhaps birth control pills, so they would not have to deal with both pregnancies, and venereal diseases from each other.

Therefore, the words such as: fornication, adultery, or even the big word "sin" lose their meaning totally even though the meaning of the words does not really change, but they would act in all cases as if there is no value on the meaning of these words, just for the fact their behavior is contrary to these words. "Safe sex", according to the world standard, does not guaranty safety at all because first, security begins always within the boundary of the law. No one is, or will ever be safe outside of the law, the law is fundamentally existed to protect, so that one can be at peace within himself. Second, security is the applying of the law that keeps one on the track which also gives one the ability to involve within the boundary of the law sets before him freely with no room for failure, or regret, and guilt whatsoever.

For example, the security that was placed around Adam and Eve in the garden of Eden was lifted, because they overstepped their boundary regarding the law of God that said: "Behold I have given you every herb bearing seed, which is upon the face of the earth, and every tree, in the which is the fruit of a tree yielding seed; to you it shall be for meat. And the Lord commanded the man, saying, of every tree of the garden thou mayest freely eat: But of the tree of the knowledge of good and evil, thou shalt not eat of it: for in the day that thou eatest thereof thou shalt surely die" **Gen.1:29-2:16-17.**[16] The security, that Adam and Eve were able to enjoy in the Garden of Eden, came from their obedience to the law, and their willingness not to eat the fruit that God told them to. Had they not touched the fruit they would still have been here today alive, and consequently, because of their disobedience to God's law, we all now are going to die one way, or another.

Another example, suppose one uses a condom, or perhaps

takes birth control pills and engages himself/ herself sexually as planned, and two years have gone by, he or she is not sick from any STD, or there is no pregnancy afterward: does that mean that both he and she are safe, and if he and she are, what is it that they are safe from? I know that for the most part, it is easy for all of us to rationalize when we come face to face with the law; we tend to usually go around it, come up with excuses instead of obeying it really, and enjoy the security that comes with it. For this reason, we put ourselves in danger and others also just like Adam and Eve did when they were in the Garden of Eden. The odd there is for a man or a woman to catch a venereal disease can be one in a million, or perhaps one out three I don't know, that is not the issue here, the issue here is that "safe sex" is not the idea of finding out ways to get away with it just to enjoy a little sexual pleasure for awhile, but it is in effect the abiding foundation that keeps us all safe, even though we may have to endure hardship to preserve it, but it will be worth it, because it is not really about us, but rather it is all about God who wants it that way.

When we all accept His way, pleasure, joy, security, and peace will come one day abundantly. I am sure if Adam and Eve had an opportunity to repeat their lives in the garden of Eden after the fact that their violation to God's word cost them their lives and ours, they would have done it differently, they would have done it the way God wanted it exactly without a second thought, but unfortunately we are continuing in the same footsteps of Adam and Eve by disobeying God, even though we have the knowledge of what happened both in the past with those who've been disobedient to God's law, and what will happen with those who are being disobedient to God's law such as those practicing sexual immorality.

Friend, the beauty of sex is truly an opportunity to be obedient to God's law with the benefit of being safe in these environments both physically and spiritually. God created us all as sexual human being, as I mentioned before, we are all the product of sexual relation, which explains the reality that apart from Adam and Eve, the rest of us all over the world would not be here if it weren't for sex. So, God wants us to have sexual relation, but only according to the way He designed it for us. A farmer would not go harvesting his crops after spending hundreds of dollars when he knows it is not harvest time yet. A baker will not take his cake out of the oven when he knows the cake is not baked yet. A surgeon will not walk away from the operating room while operating on a patient if he knows the surgery is not complete yet.

So, when it comes to sexual matter, God sets His standard, what makes you think you can violate it? Imagine for a moment friend to realize what God did with the disobedience of Adam and Eve in the Garden of Eden, the consequences He brought upon all mankind because of it; imagine if He were to allow the entire world to suffer because of each one of us disobedience. Do you realize how many times you've caused, and you are still causing people to suffer because of your disobedience to God's law? Yes! In reality in some way you've caused others to suffer perhaps through sexual abuse, abortion, pornography, homosexuality, or perhaps you have been a victim of others who've caused you to suffer, and as a result of all these you are depressed, you lose your self-esteem, and it has been damaged beyond repair, and on top of all that, the spiritual disability, that you cannot recover from, has crippled you from fulfilling God's given destiny for your life.

In all consideration, do not let this matter keep you away from God's protection for your life, and your future. I am sure you're smarter than that, you are going to obey God's law in all matter specifically in the matter of sexual relation, so that you can truly practice "safe sex", and not only that, you will be in fact under the wings of God's protection for the rest of your life because only and always in the obedience to the law security lies.

Perhaps you've noticed in some cultures of this world, that many would come to live together men and women in a romantic relationship, with the intent that they would practice living together before marriage, so that they would discover whether, or not they are compatible to avoid problems so to speak from their relationship. Friend, I truly believe that this is a wonderful idea to explore from a humanistic point of view, because naturally we all have the tendency to try out everything that we want to get involved with almost in every aspect of our life.

For instance, who would want to purchase a new pair of shoes without trying them on first, especially women when it comes to clothing, make ups, a new car, and even food. It is our way of life that we would not blindly associate ourselves with anything of this life without making an assessment to know the facts of that thing, the advantages and disadvantages regarding the thing we're about to invest in, so that we can make sure that we somehow manage to make the right choice every time the opportunity presents itself. We really want to use caution throughout all our life, so that we won't have to blame ourselves for the many mistakes we can potentially make if somehow, we do not test the matter at hand with the ability we possess, to know the facts, so at the end we can be truly happy.

However, since our wisdom becomes the guiding system of our lives, we quickly come to forget that there is an order to adhere to, a directive that was given from the beginning that this is the way that men and women should be in term of romantic relationship operate on the earth. We excel in keeping more the way we want to have things run in our lives regardless the standard that we should follow, which can only be our way of finding true joy, and true happiness before God Almighty, and before men. Friend when it comes to romantic relationship, with respect to the beauty of sex, it is not up for discussion, where you and I can openly decide to go about the way we want it for us, but rather the way He (God) wanted it for each one of us, since He has designed our life to be the revealing character of Himself throughout our time here on earth for His good pleasure. Unfortunately, we think we can decide to walk away from the established order that generates the very essence of who we are as His creation, by violating His principles contrarily to His purpose for each one of our lives within His creation.

Now imagine when two individuals of the opposite sexes come together in a romantic relationship to cohabit with each other with no solid commitment such as marriage, which was ordained by God, it is in effect a direct No, of rejecting God's perfect way of human relationship here on earth. It is also a way to say that God's way is not the way, but instead everyone's way is the way. Therefore, the standard of what should consistently be our way of life, regarding romantic relationship between the sexes, is eradicated in the mind of every one of the planet earth, in pursuing some other forms of living which in turn gives way to all sort of problems.

For examples, there is always going to have a constant struggle to define what is right versus what is wrong, not only that, the peace, that should be reigning among us people, is going to be forever gone, because there is going to be a wall of separation present that blocks any form of communication. Besides, when it comes to make even the smallest decision, who is to say I have the right to make it, or perhaps who is in the right position to make it, because it would seem to be fair when living in an environment where there is no perfect standard everyone has his own right to make his own decision.

Our God given book of life "The Bible" says in **Proverbs 16:25** "There is a way that seemeth right unto a man, but the end thereof are the ways of death." This particular verse from the Bible fits right in the rebellious mindset of those who intentionally reject the way of God, not only in regard of romantic relationship, but also in any other forms of relationship that reject God's way of life for the betterment of all of us He created.[17] Living together, even though it may seem or feel right at first on the premise of love so to speak before marriage, is practically an effort to undermine God's authority blatantly in order for one to rule over his/her life given by God.

It has never been alright, nor would it ever be in God's sight to condone human's fancy way of distortion regarding His word.

He has always been consistent in punishing the evil among His people and the evil doers, so that He can always maintain the state of purification and holiness, for He Himself is holy. For this reason alone, it cannot be tolerated, nor consider being alright, if the two parties agree to do anything they want to do, even though whatever they agree to do, does not align with God's word.

In many occasions you probably have seen couples who lived together for many years, and who have never been married as well, and it seemed perhaps at the time that everything was going smoothly for them in their relationship, and as well as other avenues of their lives are equally going greatly for them. This glimpse of happiness even it may be genuinely sincere or not, does not make it ok before God, because the fact of the matter is, when we do things as human beings regardless our status before Him that violate His law, these things become detrimental for our wellbeing, and we also become disobedient to His word. So, in a sense when things like that happen we trample God's standard under feet, and sort of like lift the lies up of the devil to be true and make him look good. That is exactly what has happened from the beginning with Adam and Eve when they had an encounter with him (the devil) after God told Adam to stay away from the tree of the knowledge of good and evil, and following their disobedience, we also in turn have suffered the consequences, which among them are pain, hunger, sickness, and ultimately death.

When God speaks we need to listen and obey His word, because it is in the obedience of His word we can always, I mean always find joy, contentment, happiness, peace, and rest for our time here on earth even though we are living in a world that produces only the impossible. So, the question is: How can we truly enjoy each other's company as couples in a heterosexual relationship, when we want to always be together outside the marriage relationship, which is against God's law? How can we also experience the "beauty of sex" among us when we do not want to appreciate the standard that God is given to us in our own way, which stands in opposition to

God's way? Remember always the example of Adam's disobedience to God's way, and what it means to us today, and also remember God's word to us today as it clearly tells us that "There is a way that seemeth right unto a man, but the end thereof are the ways of death".[18] If the first time it did not resonate well enough into our ears make no mistake, may it be so and better the second time around, because whether you believe it or not, there will be a day of reckoning. I trust that you are paying attention very closely.

Friend, dealing with the subject "The beauty of sex" in the twenty-first century as it were from the beginning, according to God Almighty the creator, may seem to be impartial and inconsiderate toward the present culture, and yet the modality of our involvement in His creation, as it relates to sexual activities speaks volumes to the use of God given ordinances such as: marriage, bear children, and so forth. You wonder how hypocritical this is, because sooner, or later somebody is getting married, but realistically speaking not knowing that he/she needs to fully accept the concept of marriage relationship according to God's way. Many, if not all of us, want to be romantically involved with someone else we desire, which is perfectly ok with God, but only we do not want, and need to be told by anyone else, especially by God how to go about it in the relationship.

In our mind, we do have a rather dangerous distorted view of human romantic relationship, even those who are not necessarily promiscuous to say the least, or some who only seek to enjoy life in the manner of self-discipline when it comes to such relationship. The danger that presents itself every time in our day of human relationship, particularly romantic relationship, is that we do not intentionally put our way of life into the right perspective to be safe, and to enjoy the freedom that comes with it. We sometimes rather go after a questionable ambiance that endangers our life in the name of freedom for a brief period, and in that moment of pleasure we are at the same time standing in opposition to God's law which He will subsequently punish both the evil and the evil doer.

I know that it is hard to enter this kind of mindset that God rules over everything in the affair of mankind in our present day, just for the fact, we do not understand the concept of submission to the authority, which begins to reverently submit to God, which is the highest of all authorities established. Keep in mind, the rebellious spirit, which stands against any form of authority established, gives ways to countless woes of life if not corrected, it will bring destruction to one's life, because the ways of man are always the ways of death, but only God's way brings freedom, joy, peace, and happiness.

Friend, to know freedom, happiness, and so forth, is to know God's way; any other ways are ways that lead to death. Without a doubt, that is exactly the product of the twenty-first century, since we are directly attacking the very foundation of God's law when it comes to human romantic relationship, marriage, government, and any other aspects of human's life.

By the way, when God created us, and the world we live in, He created us to have both a social relationship, and a spiritual relationship that work hand in hand with each other, so that our lives should be subject to His given laws. Social relationship means a relationship that focuses on the human level in helping, loving, sharing, and working with each other equally, mutually respecting each other, and as well as spiritually we understand God's authority in our lives by loving Him, respecting Him, obeying Him, obeying His word, and walking humbly before Him in every aspect of our lives during our time here on earth. If we do not adhere consistently to His law according to His will, make no mistakes friend, He will not overlook our disobedience regarding His laws. God is not a respecter of person: what He says in His Word He will do.

This libertine of relativism ideology of this century, where everyone does that which is right in his own eyes compare to the time of the Judges where they would do exactly the same with no regard to the law of God (**Judges 21:25**) judgment day will come for those who would stand in opposition to God's law.[19] That is the reason why for those who think they can be their own god, play by their own rule, live their life their own way, and worse of all, encourage others to follow their sick behavior will not stand innocent before God.

As I have mentioned before, marriage relationship is the only platform that God gives to all of us human being to be romantically and sexually engaged, other than that we are in violation of His word; therefore, we are going to be punished for breaking His law. So, God is not being impartial to those who obey His law, nor is He being inconsiderate to those who do not, He only wants all of us to benefit from His blessings, and the benefits that come with the obedience to His Law He prescribes to us in His word.

In God's economy there is privilege that leads to responsibility which leads also to accountability, so that there are always checks and balances in everything we say and do. Unfortunately, in this century and perhaps in many centuries before, or other centuries to come the tendency has always been to enjoy privileges with no ounce of responsibility, let alone to be accountable for our actions. God does not tolerate the laissez faire type behavior, and so should we, because when we are in alliance with Him by intentionally live our lives according to His word, that is when we can truly experience His love, His protection, His provisions, and any other blessings that come with it such as the beauty of sex.

A love for His word in compliance with His will, even in this century, that does not really appreciate God's plan for our lives, will lead us to prosperity, abundance, greatness, power, riches, and life everlasting, but if at anytime we will go in opposition to His word as we continue to pursue our own way, it will be like we are digging our own grave. Remember always "There is a way that seemeth right unto a man, but the end thereof are the ways of death" **Prov. 16:25.**[20]

There has been an incident that happened so long ago about a man called "Onan" in the Bible whose life has been cut short because he has been meticulously deceitful toward his brother's wife sexually, so God had to slew him. The incident was, according to God's law commonly known as (the Levirate law) when a man marries a woman in those days, if the man dies before he can have children with his wife, his younger brother is automatically to marry his widow, so that he would bring forth children, or seed for his older brother (**Deut. 25:5-10**).[1]

In the case of Onan, the younger brother of Er, he did not want to have children with his older brother's wife, so when the time came to know his brother's wife after marrying her in the process of having their sexual relation, he spilled the juice so to speak on the ground to prevent him from having a child with his wife for his brother Er, which was also a way for him to disconnect with tradition regarding with this single law (**Gen. 38:1-10**).[2]

This story of the Bible comes to mind to share with you some very important and simple principles regarding the development of this topic "No more sex". The topic "No more sex" in this segment of the book is going to be viewed in the light of God's perfect word, the Bible, as our guide to lead us in the right context of such relationship in helping us to make an informed decision about sexual relation both before marriage and outside the marriage relationship. It is my sincere belief that both men and women of our days can live a pure and holy life, if by God's grace they are willing to try to put into practice these following four principles. They are: God's sovereignty over our sexual desire: Do not allow your personal feelings to get in the way of God's perfect will for your life: Do not make God's means of blessings to become God's means of judgment to you, and Genesis 38:8' principles.

1. RECOGNIZE GOD'S SOVEREIGNTY OVER OUR SEXUAL DESIRE.

It is God's desire for you and me to have a pure and safe sexual relation with the appointed partner for life in the proper context of it, but not in our own way to do so, that is why He says "Wherefore they are no more twain, but one flesh. What therefore God hath joined together, let not man put asunder" Matt.19:6.[3] this verse gives clear understanding to God's provision for our sexual desire. Number one: it says: "Wherefore they are no more twain, but one flesh" which means the oneness in the flesh happens in marriage relationship in the proper context of sexual relation according to God's way of two people of the opposite sexes to be involved as such. So "No more sex" becomes paramount both sides of your life before and outside a marriage relationship. It is not an impossible conclusion, it is in effect a winning situation, because there should be no sexual contact whatsoever before joining with your partner for life, or no more sexual contact also with someone else besides your given partner for life while, or outside your marriage relationship.

The starting point begins of a pure and a holy sexual relation the moment you are to join in holy matrimony with someone of the opposite sex. It really does not matter whether you had previous sexual contacts or not, the holy way, or God's way of sexual relation, although you will still have scars, guilt, regrets, or maybe side effects of those previous sexual relations, begins the moment you make up your mind to say: "No more sex" where you will enter a new way of thinking regarding such relationship which also open doors to great potential opportunities, and blessings throughout the rest of your life. "No more sex" is not a burden to carry along life's way, nor should it be viewed that way, because even though there are going to be challenges, hardship, and temptation along the way, the good news is, God provides by making a way to escape. "there hath no temptation taken you, but such as is common to man: but God is faithful, who will not suffer you to be tempted above that ye are able; but will with the temptation also make a way to escape, that ye may be able to bear it" **I Cor. 10:13**.[4]

It is emphatically God's perfect way to free you from the struggle of the same degree in the mind as it were in the body sexually, to enter the platform that God has prepared for you, the marriage relationship, even if it is the only reason to flee sexual impurity. "And this I speak for your own profit; not that I may cast any snare upon you, but for that which is comely, and that ye may attend upon the Lord without distraction. But if a man think that he behaveth himself uncomely toward his virgin, if she pass the flower of her age, and need so require, let him do what he will, he sinneth not: let them marry" **I Cor. 7:35-36**.[5] So what is a man, or a woman to do? It is for you to acknowledge God's sovereignty over your sexual desire, and that He has put it in you, and for you to access it in the proper context of life to be pure before Him.

The story that's depicting the life of Onan during his sexual encounter with his wife teaches you and me even though Onan was somewhat right to decide whom to have kids with naturally, but in God's eyes he was wrong because God gave the law, He set the standard, but Onan was careless about it, he should have responded obediently to do what God wanted him to do which was to bear seed for his older brother ER. Was it that difficult for him to do? No! He just did not want to do it for his own selfish reason. Keep in mind, every time someone would stand in opposition to God's law, or His way, there are always consequences that follow, and the same blessings will follow when someone obeys his law.

2. DO NOT ALLOW YOUR PERSONAL FEELINGS TO GET IN THE WAY OF GOD'S PERFECT WILL FOR YOUR LIFE.

In Onan case, he has allowed his personal feelings to dictate his decision, one which cost him his very life, because he thought he could get away with the trick that he made when he was with his wife Tamar in the secret. God saw what he did; He slew him because his action displeased God greatly. He would have been a great asset in God's plan of redemption for mankind, if he had not done this wicked thing in the sight of the Lord. Nevertheless, his action did not stop God from continuing the process of His redemptive plan of which Tamar became one the women in the lineage of the Messiah, Jesus Christ. Unfortunately, Tamar instead of marrying Shelah Judah's youngest son as she supposed to, according to this particular law (Levirate law), she married her father in law Judah, and bore him two sons which their names were Pharez, and Zarah (**Gen.38:18, 29-30**).[6] And with Pharez Judah's son, God maintained the blood line all the way up to his fourteenth generation which was "Jacob who beget Joseph the husband of Mary of whom was born Jesus, who is called the Christ" **Matt. 1:2, 3, 16-17**.[7]

Now the question to bring to light regarding Onan's mess is, what did he have to lose if he went along with God's plan to marry his brother's wife, and bore him seed? The obvious answer is absolutely nothing, because the fact of the matter was, he would have enjoyed it to be with his wife in the proper context of marriage, where eventually he would have brought forth children with her, which would have also continued God's mandate to be fruitful and multiply **Gen. 1:28**.[8] That is why for the more reason we should not under any circumstance violate God's law which can be detrimental for our lives when we disobey; but when we obey, God's favor will be upon us to carry out His plan throughout all generations.

What a privilege! So, you see friend, your feeling can never accomplish God's will in your life, it will always get in the way of God's working through you, and it will always be a hindrance for you from experiencing God's blessings, and ultimately you will always be sad, miserable because of your feeling. Therefore, when it comes to God's working in your life; feelings should be out of the question, and let the word of God be the guiding light that can carry you through even though there may be mountains to climb, valleys to cross, high and low roads, you can rest assured you will make it ultimately in the Father's hands to where He wants you to be.

Because of Onan's disobedience friend, it seemingly looked like that there was a possibility that the coming of the Messiah would be delayed, or postponed, or perhaps not happened at all, since God wanted, through the blood line of Judah, the Messiah would come. However, we understand that God has the helm of the universe, and all the circumstances surrounded it in His hands, and for those of us who know the Lord we are at peace for the fact we know that God can also use the same circumstances and manipulate them for His pleasure, and also for the benefit of His own people "And we know that all things work together for good to them that love God, to them who are the called according to His purpose" **Rom. 8:28.**[9] That is the reason for which we should not allow our feelings to be in the way of God's doing His work in our lives, especially when we already received His revelation clearly such as the case of Onan, in knowing what to do, and what not to do, so that we can avoid being in conflict with His law which can result to a premature death, as so it was with Onan. This principle teaches us to always be at peace with God no matter what our feelings may be, and more importantly when it comes to something as valuable as our sexual desire.

3. DO NOT MAKE GOD'S MEANS OF BLESSINGS TO BECOME GOD'S MEANS OF JUDGMENT TO YOU.

There is an old saying that says: "What you don't know cannot hurt you" that is to say, the ignorance of a thing can sometimes be good to your advantage as oppose to what you know can hurt you greatly, if mishandle inappropriately.[10] Onan knew what was asked of him to do with his wife was God's way, but he purposely rejected it in order to promote his own agenda in spite of what he knew the right thing to be. He deliberately sabotaged God's plan not only for himself, but also for the rest of his family in not honoring the memory of his older brother ER, as well as fulfilling his obligation regarding such law of God (Levirate law). In **James**

chapter 4:17 the Bible says: "Therefore to him that knoweth to do good, and doeth it not, to him it is sin." Onan was in the position to honor God by doing that which he knew was good, but instead he cowardly executed his liberty to disobey God's law regarding his duty. Therefore, God did not hesitate to pour out His judgment upon him because he broke His law.[11]

The same it is going to be no different for all of us in our society today, as we seek to exercise our liberty to be involved in any sort of sexual immorality as we see fit, in purposely overstepping the boundaries that God lay before us around sexual activities. He will not hesitate to pour out also His judgment upon us, so that we will know primarily that He is God, and secondly, what He says, He means it. Onan did not have to die; he knew what he was supposed to do when he was asked by his father to go in unto his brother's wife. He understood clearly his responsibility; he simply opted out of it for the benefit of his own selfish reason which ultimately brought death upon himself. The good that he knew to do he walked away from it, and it led him to the way of death because of his own way. The Bible teaches that "The wages of sin is death ..." **Rom. 6:23**.[12] Onan got what was coming to him because he sinned, he was supposed to be God's recipient of His blessings, if only he had accepted the opportunity of being with his older brother's wife as a privilege to accomplish God's purpose in his life.

Since he decided not to go according to God's way, he not only lost his life, but he also lost the awesome opportunity to a lifetime of service. We who are come after Onan will always remember him as the one that God slew unlike others in the Bible that God tremendously blessed for their obedience such as: Joseph, David, Jacob, Joshua, Salomon, Job to name a few.

As you are living your life today in this twenty-first century, if God were to name a few names as examples of those who are faithfully obeying His law of the Bible by purposefully working to uphold His truth, would your name be mentioned, or would you be among those He will slew because of your constant disregard for

His law? The advice from this principle is this: don't be like Onan was, but be instead what he should be like, if you can imagine the beauty of God's blessings in his life had he obeyed.

Judah, Onan's father gave him a direct order concerning the obligation he had to his family (**Gen.38:8**).[13] Judah here represents God as he determines which direction to go in regard to God's plan of salvation for mankind, which will be unfolded later to us very clearly, but in any case, God is also speaking to us through His word in laying before us His plan as we go about our lives day by day, so that we can be safe and secure until He come to take us to the place which He had in mind for us since the beginning of time. In the meantime, He is not going to tolerate our sinful behavior; He will deal with us accordingly. That is why He says "Enter ye at the strait gate: for wide is the gate, and broad is the way, that leadeth to destruction, and many there be which go in thereat: because strait is the gate, and narrow is the way, which leadeth unto life, and few there be that find it" **Matt. 7:13-14**.[14]

Now how can we make God's means of blessings remain blessings to us? It is only on the willingness to accept God's plan as such for our lives, in not trying to alter it in any way whatsoever, and not even our way. That's the lesson of this principle we must live by no matter what.

4. GENESIS 38:8' PRINCIPLE

This principle is a three-part principle:

1. **Go in unto thy brother's wife**
2. **Marry her**
3. **Raise up seed**

Go in unto thy brother's wife was an imperative from Onan's father to him because of the validity of the law that he had to abide to. It was out of the question for him to say that is not what I want so to speak, but nonetheless, he was to respond obediently according to the words of his father.

Really, he was indeed obedient to his father because so far, he did exactly what his father has told him to do, which was to go in unto his brother's wife, except when he got to the point where he would have to fulfill his duty regarding the law of God; he went according to his own way. For this reason, God had to kill him for the same reason Adam and Eve had to die, and so do we eventually because "we all have sinned …. **Rom. 3:23**" and death is the price to pay for breaking God's law **Rom. 6:23.**[15]

I am convinced that Onan may have had in mind to pretend to go along with his father's request, in acting as if he was genuine to it, and eventually one day they will realize that either he, or she may have a medical condition for which they may not be able to have children, and then that way he will be off the hook. But little that he knew, he did not realize the institution of the law, by which he was called to fulfill, was in effect God's way to connect two families together, but more importantly, it was also part of the process He (God) would use to bring about the plan of redemption to save mankind.

Besides, Judah Onan's father would probably never know that his son was trying to trick him into believing that he had good intention toward his request, if he weren't killed by God for disobeying His law. Onan did not have and should not have to die, because he had another alternative to choose not to marry his older brother's wife as his father wished him, so that he could maintain God's law. The simple reason for the law was that Onan would keep his brother's name alive in Israel, if and according to the law, when brothers are living together in the same household for preventing the wife of the brother that dies to go out and marrying a stranger, which may not be part of any Israel tribes that does not keep the same tradition as they do (**Deut. 25:5-6**).[16]

The wife of the late brother would go up to the elders at the gate to expose him for refusing to raise up a name in Israel unto his brother. The elders would call him to have a talk with him, in finding out why he would not wish to raise a name up in Israel in the memory of his late brother. If he still changes not his position, then the elders would call onto his brother's wife in the presence of all the people gathering, that she should lose his shoe from off him, and spit in his face, because he would not build up his brother's house, and his name shall be called among his people "the house of him that hath his shoe loosed" (**Deut. 25:7-10.**[17]

God takes seriously His law, and the consequences that pertain to it, when the law is broken by any individual which in turn directly questions His character. In the case of Onan, it was not simply a request from his father to execute, but it was also the very word of God that he (Judah) wanted to implement in the lives of his people, so that he could reflect God's character to them, so that they could have a culture of life that would work in harmony with God's will in relationship with them day by day. The "Go in unto thy wife" was supposed to be a brand new day for Onan, the beginning of a brand new life for him and his wife together, but unfortunately it was a last day for him, and at the same time he caused Tamar his wife to be a widow for a second time around, which he left her in grief, pain, shame, for the fact her father in law might have thought that something could be seriously wrong with her, since two of his own children have been dead while married to her.

As a matter of fact, Judah was so certain that the deaths of his two sons could somehow have something to do with her, he would ask her to remain a widow at her father's house until his third son shelah be old enough to marry her, but really the reason was to protect his last son from being dead like his other two sons in the hand of Tamar his daughter in law (**Gen. 38:11**).[18] The lesson that you and I should learn from this principle so far is, that we are not above the law to think that we can get away with it any way we want to with no consequences that follow, but we are all subjects to God's law regarding, or regardless the specifics. God loves us so much, but He loves His law even much more "Heaven and earth shall pass away, but my words shall not pass away" (**Matt.24:35**).[19]

In my opinion, I believe Onan did not love his brother's wife as he should, I think he would have wanted to go out and find his own woman as we all would want to do, so that we could enjoy more the potential mate for the rest of our lives. In our present day, we realize that certain key ingredients in the making of a relationship romantically speaking, are not being considered, such as parents should be the ones who should decide whom to consider spending time with after seeking God's direction concerning first, the family he/she is from. Secondly, they would interview the one they might think is the one in laying out the ground rules of courtship accompanied with close supervision as the both parties are getting to know each other. Not only that, they would be strictly vigilant to protect their children from any types of sexual reference and impurity, should they notice some inappropriate touching, or kissing that could lead to irreparable emotional damages, and spiritual sorrows for the rest of their lives.

So, Onan had regrets in his life because, if his older brother did not die, he would not feel the need to fulfill his family tradition. He felt like he was trapped into doing something that he was not ready for, and yet at the same time he did not have the courage to openly express his feelings toward the obligation for which he was called for. God, in His omniscience, did not accept Onan's excuses, but applied the penalty for his transgression against His law, where it will be known to all generations the message that God is perfect in His ways, He will not tolerate sin because of His character.

Unfortunately, today we are still seeing manifestation of law breaking among our young people when it comes to romantic relationship. It seems as if there are no boundaries as to how they can make themselves regretfully useful at the attention to their lustful desires with each other, all in the name of love, so to speak. The fear of the Lord, that should be in place in each of their heart, is not there anymore, for the fact mostly, there are no more parents around either. And if they are around, they do not act like it, because of some lame unfounded excuses to be able to say: "It was not my fault because of such and such reason fill in the blank". Therefore, the rule of parenting, that was given to them by God, has been vanished away, and has been replaced by whatever else they could possibly put their hands on, to sort of like band aid the problem, so that they can say that they love their children by giving them what they want.

For example, I have seen and heard parents who would come along side their children supporting them in their wrongdoings because the lie out there was "I can't stop them from doing what they are doing whether smoking, drug, alcohol, sex and other things, I might as well support them, or help them to protect themselves". I have one time witnessed a parent with his teenage son come to a local convenient store to buy him condoms, so that he would be safe from getting STD even though he could not stop him from having sex, so the least he thought he could do was to buy him condoms. I'd say, what about being a parent to him by beginning to lay the ground rules?

I think many times parents would say, they cannot do anything about their kids sex, drugs, alcohol's problems, is because after they have watched their kids to become, or to turn into something they barely recognize, which at the moment it seems to be too late to reverse the situation with them while the situation is too far deterioted, that when they see it too late for them to do something about it, because all they have done to fix the problem was to work backwards, and they forget that it was solely their responsibility "To train up a child in a way he should go: and when he is old, he will not depart from it" (**Prov. 22:6**).[20]

The principle here is to start the training at the earliest possible of their age, in other word when they still have fear for you, so that as they are growing up they will still have fear for you, and not only that, they will be ready to be introduced to the Lord while their heart has been stirred up with God's word "Thy word have I hid in mine heart, that I might not sin against thee" (**Ps. 119:11**).[21] The whole reason, that Onan's father wanted his son to respond obediently to the law of God, was because his primary focus was to teach his kids God's way, so that he would help protect his kids' souls from destroying, in an effort to continue the legacy of serving God that was passed on onto them, so that they, in turn when they would become older, would in no doubt love and follow God's way throughout the rest of their lives. For God wants us to "Obey them that have the rule over you and submit yourselves: for they watch for your souls, as they that must give account, that they may do it with joy, and not with grief: for that is unprofitable for you" **Heb. 13:17**.[22]

2. Marry her is the second step, and a very important step in the human romantic relationship as it is given to us by the Lord. It is in effect a door where two people of the opposite sexes can enter a lifetime covenant with each other until death due them apart. According to God's way, this is marriage, it is not a man with a man, not it is a woman with another woman. If you notice the instruction from Onan's father "marry her" meaning he called upon his son Onan (male) to join in covenant relationship traditionally with Tamar (female) so that they could cleave to each other in recognizing that their union in holy matrimony, was of God not of man, and at the same time they would be models among the habitants of the earth in their days of what should be a representation of God's awesome way of romantic involvement. That is the reason why because Onan was in some way trying to change that which God explicitly wanted him to do in marriage relationship, he did not do it, consequently he was eliminated upon the face of the earth without hesitation.

Now we probably will never know whether Onan made it to Abraham's bosom, or not until we will get there with God. The fact of the matter was, he did not believe God, therefore he may not be part of God's family, and that is mostly the essence of being obedient to God's word because His word is the rod by which He measures our faith in Him "so then faith cometh by hearing, and hearing by the word of God" **Rom. 10:17**.[23] By the way, it is not uncommon among us today that people can receive their due rewards in accordance to their actions. For instance, we know if an individual run the red lights the police will automatically serve him with a ticket for violating the law. The same an employee from any company is deliberately violating the company's policies after the fact he has been instructed about the specifics, he will get either reprimanded written up, or fired, because his action is contradicting the company's trust. Therefore, he will not be tolerated; he will be dealt with according to the company's law. So, it is for us human beings, even though we have the free will to exercise our choice, but God has the ultimate word, what He says it will stand, no one can, or should question His authority.

When Onan was called to marry his older brother's wife, it was God's will for him, because God had a specific plan if only he were to respond obediently, just like He (God) has a plan for all of us because He says: "For I know the thoughts that I think toward you, saith the Lord, thoughts of peace, and not of evil, to give you an expected end" **Jeremiah 29:11**.[24] The lesson from this principle is this: God has always something better for you than what He asks from you. What God had in store for Onan was not simply to be with his older brother's wife, besides there was not anything shameful about it, because whatever he would do, he would do it within the boundary of the law which gave him the freedom to do so, but in order for Onan, according to God's plan, he had to go through the process of " Go in unto thy brother's wife" then "marry her" so that "And raise up seed to thy brother" **Gen.38:8** which is to come after which consequently also will fulfill God's plan in his life as He saw fit to him.[25] That is why it is so vitally important to let God have His way with us because for this simple reason "Know ye that the Lord He is God: it is He that hath made us, and not we ourselves: we are His people, and the sheep of His pastures" **Ps.100:3**.[26] When God requires anything of us we should always be ready for Him.

Two examples from the Bible: one is when Jesus was about to enter the city of Jerusalem at Bethpage and Bethany, He specifically delegated two of His disciples and instructed them "Go your way into the village over against you: and as soon as ye be entered into it, ye shall find a colt tied, whereon never man sat; loose him, and bring him. And if any man say unto you, why do ye this? Say ye that the Lord hath need of him; and straightway he will send him hither" **Mark 11:2-3.** You've noticed from this passage both the donkey and his owner responded obediently to the Lord, and not only that, Jesus did not need permission from the donkey's owner to use him, He simply said "That the Lord hath need of him" with that in mind, this example puts us right in the context of God tremendous power and sovereignty over everything He created.[27] So who is Onan to say that he does not want to do this, or who are we to say that's not the way we want it? Such attitude before God will always be resulted to God's judgment, or death.

Since He created all, He has the right to ask of us whatever His heart desires. "All things were made by Him (GOD); and without Him was not any thing made that was made" **John1:3**. "And to make all men see what is the fellowship of the mystery which from the beginning of the world hath been hid on God, who created all things by Jesus Christ" **Eph3:9** and also "For by Him (JESUS) were all things created that are in heaven, and that are in earth, visible and invisible, whether they be thrones, or dominions, or principalities, or powers: all things were created by Him and for Him" **Col.1:16**. It should be in our best interest that we understand the character of God no matter what our world view may be, because in the end, we will all stand before Him to give an account, for not only what we did with our life, but also how we responded to God's call through His Son Jesus Christ whom He has sent unto this earth to redeem us.[28]

The other example is also when Jesus was about to have the last supper with His disciples in the upper room before He went to the cross. Jesus sent again two of His disciples and He said "Go ye into the city, and there shall meet you a man bearing a pitcher of water: follow him. And wheresoever he shall go in, say ye to the good man of the house, the Master saith, where is the guest chamber, where I shall eat the Passover with my disciples? And he will shew you a large upper room furnished and prepared: there make ready for us" **Mark 14:13-15**. So, you see friend, twice Jesus delegated two of His disciples to execute His wishes which had great meaningful results during and after the ministry of Jesus upon the earth, both in His life and in the life of mankind in general.[29]

The common denominator, of these two examples, is the fact that both man of each example responded obediently to Jesus' request even though neither one of them had no previous encounter with Jesus. These two examples were divinely inspired and preordained even before the beginning of time, so that they would, for us mankind, be lessons to teach us not only obedience, but also the sovereign power of God over His all creation.

3. Raise up seed is the third, and ultimate step of the principle, which indicates the readiness of a transitional period between a father and his son, which is the next generational leader of the Judah's family. Suffice it to say that this transition was also a door of opportunity to bring God's righteous way to the land of Canaan, since we know both Shuah and Tamar were not part of any tribes of Israel (**Gen.38:2,6**). They were accepted into the family of God because they had welcomed with open arms Judah and his custom of his faith as well. That was one of the reasons that showed Tamar was okay with marrying ER, the second son of Judah, which was also evidence that she had embraced the Jewish tradition regarding the levirate law (**Gen. 38:8-9; Deut. 25:5-10**).[30]

However, raise up seed according to God's economy would be identified in everybody's mind as the third phase of the **Genesis 38:8'** principle, meaning that the first two have been fulfilled. And it is in fact God's precedence commanded to us to follow to be compliant with Him, in pursuing a romantic relationship with the opposite sex. This third part of the principle gives the satisfaction of acknowledging where you are at, to continue with no guilt and shame the work of preparing good grounds as the seeds are being planted in them, so they can blossom with the expectation of great harvest with plenty because of dedicated works in alignment with righteousness.

At this point, a new chapter is introduced to everyone in the family, where you will have to inculcate, and the implementation of God's righteous living in the mind of the ones that will be called your children, so that in the effort to reproduce good seeds to pass on to the next generations to come. It is vitally important that we seek God's way as a family, and individually for that matter, because in seeking God's way it will help putting down evil and destroying wickedness from our world. "Righteousness exalteth a nation: but sin is a reproach to any people" **Prov. 14:34.**[31]

Raise up seed is a tremendous opportunity to work for God, and yet it can be stressful and a delicate task in standing in opposition to the world, that not only is the archenemy of God, but also hates the friends of God, and the work they do to bring about justice, righteousness in everything they do, and the spread of each one of them throughout their lives upon the earth. With that in mind, for those of us who are God's people we have the obligation to reflect the light of Jesus Christ, and His gospel to the creation of God in this vicious, and wicked world. **Genesis 38:8'** principle mirrors God's perfect character as it stands regarding human romantic relationship, so that it can be the pattern to follow, when dealing with issues as such to have a panoramic view of His will for mankind, both blessings, and curses, depending on how His words are being handled.

Besides, this principle is alluding with the great commission that Jesus gives to (**Matt.28:19-20; Mark 16:15-16**). all of us who are friends of His from the books of the gospel "Go ye therefore, and teach all nations baptizing them in the name of the Father, and of the Son, and of the Holy Ghost. Teaching them to observe all things _ Go ye into all the world and preach the gospel to every creature. He that believeth and is baptized shall be saved, but he that believeth not shall be damned".[32] In both **Genesis 38:8** and the other two passages of the gospel, we are commanded to "Go" which is a command from God, which gives a precise and clear understanding that we are to take action toward something that He wants us to do. In the Genesis passage it says: "Go in unto thy brother's wife" in the New testament passages it also says "Go ye therefore and teach all nations…. Go ye into all the world" which explains we do have both the command and the place. Then it says in the Genesis passage "And marry her" and in the New testament passages it says "teach all nations … preach the gospel" which explains in one hand marry her is making an alliance, in other word, to enter a covenant relationship for ever, which in the other hand, as we teach, and preach the gospel to the world, we are opening the door to an eternal covenant relationship with God through Jesus Christ His Son who is also the groom of the church, and is in fact the bride of Christ.

Finally, in the Genesis passage, it says: "Raise up seed to thy brother" and the New testament passage it says: "He that believeth shall be saved" which gives us a clear picture of God's love for His people in establishing ways for all of us to maintain a relationship with Him. In the Old Testament's days, He made it possible through the sons of Jacob, or the children of Israel to continue to multiply, and replenish the earth in keeping the promise He had made to Abraham through his son Isaac in a physical sense of the promise (**Gen.12:1-3; 15:1-18**), but in the New Testament's days, He extended His hands to us the rest of the world through the shedding blood of His only begotten Son Jesus Christ on the cross in the spiritual sense of the promise, to bring forth a people for His own as He commands us to go throughout **Matt. 28:19-20; Mark 16:15-16; Titus 2: 11-14** the world, to preach the gospel to every creature. So, all we must do is apply the blood to our lives in the name of Jesus.[33]

Naturally in all walks of life we all have come to be familiar to boasting physically, mentally, spiritually, so that we can assuredly arrive to attain goals that have been set before us. Those goals that we so long desire to attain may be sometimes some of the most fulfilling things to accomplish in one's life, also they may be some of the most ridiculous ones to seek after depending on the need motivating those goals. Yet in any area of life, where boasting is the vehicle moving us from one side of the goals to the next despite of our efforts, we all acquire always the same technical support to succeed, which is the assistance of "Tools", they are very important to help accomplishing a task. Since God told Adam that he would have to sweat to get his bread (**Gen.3:19**) He has made it a law for all of us who've come after that, we would not get anything just by the command of the sound of our voice, but instead we would have to continuously use tools in all walks of life to accomplish something with purpose and benefits.[1] Therefore, it is with great pride that God gave us sexual relation, mainly as a tool, to accomplish something else of greater significance in the program of all our lives.

This built in tool, that God has given to all of us human beings, has purposes for which God decided to include it in our physiology make up, and which also has tremendous power to help define the reality of our existence in accordance to God's word, and consequently, it can be detrimental in relationship to each other gender, if somehow we neglect to make use of it, in opposition of the author's original intention. With that in mind, let's talk about sex, its purpose mainly in human being lives, and how it relates to us all in our day to day relationship with the opposite sex.

It is of utmost importance to consider joining God's side of the equation, because once a decision is made in violating God's law of sexual involvement, it is irreversible, except given the thought of what we know God can do will keep us safe from His wrath regarding His law. Notice, in God's mind He wants us all to experience wisdom, so that we can also be all in the center of His will, He said "Wisdom is the principal thing; therefore, get wisdom: and with all thy getting get understanding. Exalt her, and she shall promote thee: she shall bring thee to honour, when thou dost embrace her. She shall give to thine head an ornament of grace; a crown of glory shall she deliver to thee. Hear, O my son and receive my sayings; and the years of thy life shall be many, I have taught thee in the way of wisdom; I have led thee in the right paths. When thou goest, thy steps shall not be straitened, and when thou runnest, thou shall not stumble" **Prov. 4:7-12.**[2]

In God's economy, He only operates from an eternal perspective, where His love is eternal, His grace is eternal, His salvation is eternal, and so forth, therefore we need to assume that the purpose of Him giving us sex is as well eternal, because in the sight of God, when two people of the opposite sexes are joined in marriage, God says: "They are no more twain, but one flesh. What therefore God hath joined together; let no man put asunder" **Matt.19:6**. So we can safely say, since God does not want us to get sexually involved outside the marriage relationship, the purpose of sex is for an eternal covenant before both each other, and God Almighty.[3] And it is through this particular relationship that one can truly experience a glimpse of God's amazing love for mankind. Jesus teaches that a house that is built upon sand won't stand. When the wind blows, the flood comes, the house will collapse, but if it is built upon a rock a sure foundation, then it will stand when troubled times come, and so is marriage that is built upon the rock of the word of God will last forever, because the rock is Jesus Christ (**Matt.7:24-27**) which by the way, is the lamb that God sacrificed to bring us back to Him forever.[4]

So, it is impossible for us human beings to love one another in our own way, because by nature we are all wicked, let alone to have a covenant relationship forever such as marriage, but with God's love within ourselves, we can love one another, and we can attempt to enter marriage covenant relationship with the opposite sex that lasts forever. The directives, that God gives to couples of opposite sexes in marriage relationship, are first "Husbands love your wives, and wives submit yourselves to your own husbands" **Col.3:18-19; Eph.5:21-26**. Besides, being in a marriage covenant relationship, it is in effect God's way of demonstrating in all human level His love for mankind as we can see it pictured through Christ's relationship with the church (**Eph. 5:25**). This love Christ has for His church is a pure, sincere, genuine love, which was authenticated by His dying on the cross for solely of reconciling a sinner to a Holy God, in establishing a mutual love relationship between the two forever.[5]

Therefore, as we look at sex, it is so much more in effect to reconnect the male man in his proper form as he once was with the "Rib" that God intentionally detached from him at his indigenous existence, whereas he will be complete once that lost rib is found. And so, sex becomes paramount particularly in the life of the male gender, which in turn is in quest of finding his lost piece of his physiology make up that is somewhere out there, without which he is incomplete to accomplish God's primary purpose, which is to be fruitful and multiply (**Gen.1:28**).[6]

This mystery that was divinely presented to us by God Almighty in the garden of Eden, when He took Adam's rib for solely the reason of bringing Adam another person of the same kind, but different gender, defines totally through the sexual relation with which makes him whole again both physically and spiritually. By the way, Adam was with one woman throughout the rest of his life, even though he would not have made sense for him to be with another woman, since he was basically the grandfather of any other woman that came from his children. The principle here to learn from is; that every man should consider himself as Adam to be with one woman for the rest of his life, considering that he is by default the grandfather of any other woman after that he meets.

Besides, God had only used, notice "A rib" singular to bring forth a woman (singular) to Adam. God did not take several ribs from him which would allow him to look for his ribs (plural) out there, which in turn would give man today the same opportunity to do likewise, but rather man should keep in mind he only has to look for that one and only rib out there, and once that rib is found his search is also over, because the focus according to God's way has always been, and continuing to be today one man for one woman as it is one woman for one man. The idea, for a man to be with many women, is outrageous simply because he is stealing other men's women, and at the same time he cannot marry multiple women at the time, he only can marry one in accordance to the law of the land and as well as God's.

Understand friend, the reason, we human beings ought to accept things the way God sees them, is because everything will fall in the right place to fulfill God's purpose in each of our lives to honor Him even through, or with the things He intentionally gives to us according to His sovereign will. Sex is not a toy to play with, any time we feel like, but rather a tool for God to use in our lives to honor and glorify His name as He wants. As we look at sexual relation from outside the context of marriage relationship, between a man and a woman, the purpose of it, is at war against the original purpose of such relation the way God intended it to be, for the fact primarily, it does not bring honor to God, but to man. It is considered by many a successful tool to acquire sensual pleasures, as being in direct contact with the very best of nature's gift (woman) in seeking to free themselves from regulatory structures, with which maintains the foundational integrity of the human life in relationship between the sexes, particularly a romantic relationship. This rational, that they are not defined by God's purpose when it comes to sexual relation, puts them in opposition to the normalcy of life of such relation before God and before man, and is undermining the very foundation that brought them here in the first place.

Therefore, we need not to engage ourselves into something we know for sure will destroy our own existence, because it will, if change is not made as soon as possible. God gives instruction to us particularly men not to give our strength unto women, (plural)

(**Proveb.31:3**) in other word, God wants us to stay pure not to waste ourselves into wrong sexual pleasures because "For by means of a whorish woman a man is brought to a piece of bread: and the adulteress will hunt for the precious life" **Prov. 6:26**.[7] It seems that the imperative here is to give up one's desire for sexual pleasures, that is not God's way in the interest to protect the human race in such manner, which in my opinion is as equally important for all of us as to drink clean and pure water for health reason. There is no debate that it is not a matter of preference whether all of us human beings, or not need to consume clean water to stay healthy.

It is everybody's goal to do so, and not only that, if anybody would dare to say dirty water is good for your health, and perhaps in some way would promote this agenda, chances are the reaction toward this individual with such agenda would be chaotic to say the least, because the fact of the matter is, no one wants to digest dirty water in his system. So, why is it different when it comes to practice sexual purity? Why can't we employ the same principle for the same reason that we need to drink clean water in our life for sexual practice? I truly believe there should be no reason to act indifferently in our sexual practices which consequently if we do so, we pay greatly with our health, which by the way, it is the intention of the God Almighty to save us from the product of our sexual impurity, but not so much that He wants to punish us, nor does He want to impose His will on us to navigate our lives in any direction He sees fit.

At the contrary, if anything that God will do, is to impose Him on us, if He wanted to do so, He would have done it from the beginning with the very first family Adam and Eve, and we wouldn't certainly be in the mess we are in today, whereas we are trying so hard to find our way out. That is the more reason that we really need to pay attention to God's law, for it is the only way humanity can survive the downfall of its own demise in the sexual arena. If for example, couples outside God's law of sexual relation encounter difficulties, such as conflict of interest, or incompatibility of character, or perhaps lack of respect for one another in their relationship, these signs can be great assets in discovering a balanced relationship among themselves, if they turn to God for guidance. But unfortunately, if they do not turn to God's way, instead they seek counsel from none God fearing marriage counselor professional, as they would normally do, so that they may work on their problems with the hope to restore the relationship.

The fact of the matter is, because relationship is both at the same time physical and spiritual, working on the physical with a professional can only do just that, but the other aspect will be neglected so bad that it will in fact expose, I presume the sentiment toward each other, also toward their relationship that is potentially on the brink of collapsing if not handled properly.

To avoid this kind of situation in a marriage relationship, even for those who are not in God's side, even them can also find real intimacy in applying God's principles for heterosexual relationship, in letting Him to be the God of their everything including their sex life always. So, what would happen if somehow, more specifically the wife feels neglected by her husband sexually? The answer to that question is given in part in the book "No more Headaches" written by DR. Juli Slattery, a Christian psychologist that "having sex is a natural physiological practice. People have figured it out how to do it on their own since the beginning of time". She also says that "although sex "just happens" a dynamic sex life does not; without effort, time, and attention, sex can easily and quickly become mundane and predictable, and can even turn into dreaded necessity to place on the to-do list". She goes on to say; in order to have a solid intimacy, works need to be done from both parties in the relationship such as "sex as a gift, an interest, an ability that can be cultivated. You will never be a great cook unless you experiment with new recipes --- you will never be a great tennis player unless you take lessons and play regularly --- you will never learn to play the trumpet without hours of practice and instruction. Don't assume that sex is any different. You and your husband won't have a great sex life unless you make it a priority to actually work out intimacy together".[8]

I believe what DR. Juli is trying to convey through these wonderful thoughts, is simply whenever marriages are suffering, both members need to make it a goal to work out their differences, and other facts that may be hindrances in their relationship to focus on the big picture, which is their sacred union "Marriage" and move on in the right direction to love and cherish each other until death due them part. By the way, in the context of "the purpose of sex" viewed as a tool that God uses to bring honor unto Him, we also do not want to forget, that the blood covenant that occurs between the sexes through the initial sexual contact primarily to break the seal, which unites them both as one through the blood that is shed in there. It is exclusively by the means of this tool "sexual contact" that this unveiling divine mystery can happen, whereby mister "X" can join with miss "Y" in holy matrimony for a perpetual life together, that is indeed accepted in God's program of life.

This union is not random, or casual as many would make it to be, it is rather eternal because of the fact, it is authenticated through the breaking of the seal during sexual intercourse between the sexes for the first time. This seal represents in part the absolute proof of a female virgin, this seal medically known as the "Hymen" or "Maidenhead" has not been broken simply because she has not been involved in any sexual intercourse activities whatsoever since the day of her birth. And at the same time, because the seal remains intact prior to sexual activities, it gives her a distinctive mark that would allow her to broker a wonderful, loving, peaceful romantic relationship in marriage with the man which would find her faithful for waiting especially for him, when the blood is shed during her first sexual contact. This bloodshed there, is in effect the authenticity of a sacred union ordained by God of two families, that together join in holy matrimony who also love God dearly and are separated from the world to live for God, expressing it as a living sacrifice because of the shedding of the blood.

Needless to say, this way of God, to bring particularly two families together as He intended it to be for marriage relationship, is extremely a rare occurrence in the twenty-first century. It should not have to be a surprise, nor should it be an impossible accomplishment among ourselves human beings, if perhaps we have been given room for God in our lives, or perhaps if we have been devoted our lives to lovingly and graciously obey God's law concerning our involvement with each other gender sexually, we would be no doubt fantastically happy, and fearfully in good stand with His law in today's romantic relationship of the society. But in any case, we do not want to ignore that there are many marriages where mostly the women have been the faithful ones, which during their lives they never had any sexual relation before marriage, or perhaps there were many couples who've come together in marriage where both parties have never been sexually involved prior to their marriage, but they in fact had been sexually involved with other partners before they met each other. And there may be those who've come to marriage relationship where one party has been totally faithful since birth, where the other has had multiple sexual relations prior their union, or maybe both were living together for number of years, and even had children before they decided to tie the knot officially in marriage relationship.

The fact of the matter is, because this trend of sexual appetite among the sexes of the world, we cannot help to think, that even once, or twice prior to marriage, couples are mostly involved in some form of sexual relation even among those who call themselves born again Christians. It is not uncommon, that especially our young people to view sexual relation as no brainer, a given in any courtship relationship of our day, because they are not taught that it is not part of a courtship relationship, and that it is simply a benefit, or a blessing that comes because of being married. So, imagine then your first time what it meant for the both of you, whether you have come together, following a formal wedding ceremony, or not. Let's talk about that, shall we?

Morally speaking, we are defiant for the sole purpose of our existence, where the law of such relation that has been given to us for our own enjoyment, has been purposely swept under the rug of libertinism, to enhance one's pleasure without limit. Therefore, destructive pattern of sexual behavior began to sprout in our midst, where the moral law of God became insensitive to many, which caused them to react strongly in opposition to God's standard, that has brought them here in the first place. Those destructive patterns such as: homosexuality, lesbianism, bestiality, sexual intercourse before marriage, promiscuity, adultery, and so forth, are in effect, tangible proofs that show the heart of man how irreverently he disregards God's law in his life.

Mankind has arrived at a point in his life, where he is carelessly intimate with his own demise daily, because he does not want to follow the original model of human sexual relationship orchestrated by God our creator, through Adam and Eve our very first parents. In so doing, the line of demarcation for sexual involvement has been crossed, and consequently following that, we developed a culture of young people that are disobedient to their parents, and haters of the law of God, they also have become unaware of the reality of the God's like attributive in the society. Because of that, we cannot contain the growth multiplied of our young people sexually participated, even at the earliest age possible of their lives. It has become for them a product of necessity of life, just like it is at the same level of food, clothing, and shelter one needs to survive. And so, morality at this point is not a criterion to consider for sexual involvement, but instead, it is strictly prohibited them fulfilling their heart's desires. The question is so far: how was it the first time when one got to be sexually involved?

Aside traumatic experience one could have to describe his first time ever involved in a sexual relationship, such as: rape, sexual abuse, incest, or unpleasant sexual partners, it would not be surprising to hear that it was fabulously awesome, and no regret because it was done in its proper context intended. But for many, it is going to be rather interesting stories, because over all, they are simply results of foolish ideas mentally capitulated in exercising a form of freedom, that opened the doors of possibilities of an inevitable failed life sooner, or later.

Tradition suggests that one should weigh his option, and carefully plan his life in gearing toward success, even going against all odds, and peer pressures. As one may think, that he has it all figured out, he should also at the same time remember the alternative which brings about the moral aspect of life, centered only on God's final authority, His word. When two unmarried teenagers a boy, and a girl have come together, involving in series of sexual relations among themselves, or perhaps unmarried adults for that matter, embracing the same ritual with no regard for morality, it cries out for serious damages the likes of which, that not only physically, or emotionally deranged, but also it is spiritually at risk that can lead to an eternal lost unseen.

The first time in any given activity of one's lifetime realistically speaking, is the net worth of that individual being put in the line without reservation to acquire independence for a continual establishment to pursue with purpose. It is in effect, a well calculated effort from that individual with determination for success while exercising faith for precedence seemingly perfect. Unlike activities such as: first time learning to ride a bicycle, or perhaps having difficulties of hitting the right notes in learning an instrument for the first time, which do not seem to have major emotional attachment to them, sexual relation is both at the same time emotional, and spiritual, that manifests itself, in the physical level as expression of love. That is the reason why, one must arrange a reliable platform, the one that encompasses not only the physical, the emotional, but more importantly the spiritual, so that following this act there will be no guilt, no regret, and no violation against the law of sexual involvement.

This reliable platform is none other than "Marriage relationship". It is the only safe place where two individuals of the opposite sexes can truly enjoy themselves sexually without restriction, or any violation of the law against it, but the alternative is not reliable, and without a doubt unsure. In pursuing a relationship in such a manner without the sure platform, clearly undermines the foundation upon which to do so, but also it becomes abominable to anyone who practices it outside the marriage platform foundation that was given by the creator, in joining together the first man and the first woman at the beginning.

Friend when a young boy gets sexually involved with a young girl vice a versa just for the sole purpose of being cool, or perhaps because they love each other, what they did it's called "Sin" or in other word precisely it's called "Fornication". First, it's called "Sin" because there was a breach of trust; they in effect missed the mark, because they've come short to the standard of God. Second, it's called "Fornication" because they have done it simply differently from the platform that God placed before them. This sin is specifically attributed to those who are sexually involved before marriage, whether it is the young people, or adults for that matter. Finding them involved in such activity, they are automatically called "Fornicators" because they violated God's law of sexual involvement.

Many of you perhaps are wondering if there is even an ounce of possibility that anybody of this twenty-first century world sexual oriented, especially our young people who can go about his life without having sex for a long time before marriage. And if there is such a person either he, or she is not normal, because sex is practically handed to whosoever wants it, since it is at the reach of everybody, whether freely getting it, or paying for it. It is right here in front of you and I; how can one resist such a temptation? Truly I would be the first one to admit that it is seriously crazy out there with the high demand, and rampant sexual activities in our midst of this twenty-first century, because of the fact that social media such as: the internet, magazines, face book, movies, and some television programs, that we let invading our homes with a wrong kind of philosophy of love, causes this present culture to shape after their modality of entertainment accepted as good and normal, which consequently destroy the very foundation that was once the guiding light to our lives to a moral society safe and protected.

As of right now we certainly operate with no conviction of a moral society, because we let go that which we knew, and believed to live by as our core values, such as: the word of God to be infallible, having prayer in every aspect and branches of institution that govern our lives, and having reverence for those that are in authority over our lives, in keeping us in the right track to distinguish right from wrong, to embrace the ideology of many with an approach of pluralistic relativism mindset, especially in the area of sexual relationship, which is basically the door of your fabrication, which potentially can be used for both good and evil.

When an individual act outside the parameter of sexual relationship involvement for the first time, he opens the door basically of a disobedient life potentially for the rest of his life. He has become automatically a law breaker, which perhaps will carry on for the rest of his life. He is standing in opposition to God always as he continues breaking other laws that surround his life. Therefore, he is out there going on with a guilty conscience, hardening his heart toward God's way of life, refusing to express regrets regarding his wrongdoings, also not wanting to apply faith to God's word, and ultimately, he never repents, he dies with a rebellious heart, and ends up in Hell for all eternity.

Unfortunately, there are people out there that live their lives exactly the way I just described. They do not have a concept of right and wrong foundation, because of the fact they did not have a home that brought them up in the nurture and the admonition of the Lord; or perhaps they did have a home as such, but they did not accept it to live by. They were born lost, they lived their lives lost, and they will die eventually lost if they do not repent still.

You see my friend, an individual can be in a lost state of mind throughout the rest of his life and remain in that state the moment he allowed "sin" entering his life for the first time, regardless the theological aspect of his life if you will, a sin such as sexual relation before marriage. This sin in of itself does not send him to Hell, but the fact that he refuses to accept it as sin in his life for which he needs to repent from, the same he may continue to live his life with no regard for God's law, and at the end he dies without acknowledging that he was a sinner in need of salvation, goes to Hell. The point that I am making here is this: a rebellious heart toward God's law about anything can lead one to a total oblivion of God's sovereignty over his life where he will eventually stand in opposition to God Himself to a point where he will be almost impossible for him to repent in accepting God's grace of salvation.

Now the real issue here, whether we accept God's way, or not for this truth of our existence, is the fact that we are in any position to counter God's principle no matter what it is. It is in our safe interest that we ought to oblige in favor of God's sovereign authority over us as His creation. Because no matter what we say or do contrarily to His word, we will be always in defense, where the possibility of winning is greatly impossible. Therefore, what we need to do is simply to rely on Him for strength to overcome the challenges, and the temptations that we face constantly while keeping in mind, that He (God) is not our enemy, but the tempter, the deceiver Satan the devil is. For example, it is much easier for an individual who is not a born-again Christian, who is not a member of God's family, to involve in activities that do not hold God's standard to live by, than an individual who is a child of God. Because the one that is not of God sees Him as a restrainer each time he wants to expend his horizon of exploration, an opportune way to live life to the fullest. In fact, to the one that is of God, because he loves God, he seeks always to please Him (God) no matter the circumstance at hand, because he also knows "The fear of the Lord is the beginning of knowledge: but fools despise wisdom and instruction" **Prov. 1:7.**[9]

With that in mind, that is why the word of God makes such significant impact and difference in the lives of those who fear Him.

The word of the Lord gives knowledge and wisdom, in guiding us to go through this life. For those who fear Him (God) understand that their success depends on their obedience to God's word "For the Lord giveth wisdom: out of His mouth cometh knowledge and understanding" **Prov. 2:6**; not only that, but also they do know that there is nothing to lose in obeying God's word because "He (God) keepeth the paths of judgment, and preseveth the way of His saints" **Prov. 2:8**. Especially when it comes to practice sexual purity, it really does not matter whether you are a child of God, or not, the principle remains the same, because God punishes the sin and the sinner. He does not tolerate sin, or the practice of it in any way.[10]

As we are dealing with the subject "The purpose of Sex" we cannot address this subject based only on the understanding of our surroundings as this subject relates to us, but also it is important that we rely our hope on the one that knows it better when it comes to the practice of it among ourselves human beings, in looking through the lenses of His established words for light, and guidance.

For this cause, God, the creator warns us human beings, His creature to stay away from wrongful sexual practices that are orchestrated by the devil himself with sole purpose to destroy our lives, and ultimately our relationship with God Almighty. His warnings are consistently to keep us safe from the pawns of the devil in all aspect of our lives. The reason for it is as follow, if we have wisdom "To deliver thee from the way of the evil man (Satan), from the man that speaketh froward thing, who leave the paths of uprightness, to walk in the way of darkness; who rejoice to do evil, and delight in the frowardness of the wicked; whose ways are crooked, and they froward in their paths" **Prov.2: 12-15**. And not only God wants to keep us safe from the devil's pawns, but also, He wants to keep us pure from sexual sin of all kinds, in obeying His Words, He wants "To deliver thee from the strange woman, even from the stranger which flattereth with her words; which forsaketh the guide of her youth, and forgetteth the covenant of her God. For her house inclineth unto death, and her paths unto the dead. None that go unto her return again, neither take they hold of the paths of life. That thou mayest walk in the way of good men and keep the path of the righteous. For the upright shall dwell in the land, and the perfect shall remain in it. But the wicked shall be cut off from the earth; the transgressors shall be rooted out of it" **Prov. 2:16-22.** In being compliant with God's word, one can be spared from the judgment to come, and unfortunately if one is not, His judgment will be carried out just like He says according to **Proverbs 2:22** "But the wicked shall be cut off the earth, and the transgressors shall be rooted out of it". Our goal is to help preventing this woe from happening to you, if you continue to practice wrong kind of sexual activities.[11]

Notice, that there are always consequences following the breaking of God's law, something that is not new to the table, in looking at this issue of sexual purity from God's perspective. God requires holiness all the way for both His children, and those who are yet to be His children, according to the scriptures. Even for those who are called His children need to walk before Him according to His word, and that's what we called "**Sanctification**" so that He can be pleased, and they can be useful to Him here on earth for the advancement of the gospel of truth, which in turn can help preserving the human race, and if yet, being children of God, they are involving in the same manner as those who are not His children in sexual sins, whether before marriage "**Fornication**" or during marriage "**Adultery**" or other perverted sexual sins, God will have His way with them: because judgment begins first unfortunately, in the house of the Lord.

That is the reason why, when a child of God is found in sexual sin, automatically his relationship with his God is broken, there is no fellowship anymore because sin has put a wedge in between, and therefore, restoration needs to take place immediately through the process of "**Sanctification**". The relationship is simultaneously affected in all levels: physically, emotionally, and spiritually.

As of this moment, we all need to get a grip of ourselves, to decide how we need to respond to God's law of sexual involvement for the reason of which He has given it to us intentionally. My suggestion would be that, as we are looking within ourselves in trying to understand our responsibility toward God's law in everything, and at the same time to see God for who He is, regarding His laws and how they relate to us, to take our eyes away from those temporary pleasures that come with disobedience of God's law, so that we can see them with an eternal perspective, the way God sees them in a meaningful way. Suffice it to say, God expects us to see His creation from His perspective, that is why He gives us His laws by which we can enjoy fully that which He has created to please Him always. We should not trouble yourselves, there is no arm twisting to please, or to do God's will. It is only in the willingness of the heart from our part to know and honor Him from His word in everything we say and do.

Certainly, this may very well be a bit of a challenge for many, for we are not all members of His family, not only that, we do not all see things in the exact way according to His word. For some, they do not accept the notion of a God that created everything, let alone to believe in His word, but others they don't seem to care whether there is a God or not, they just want to do their own things their own way, and they do not want to accept the consequences they deserve sometimes. Unfortunately, the sad news is, there are consequences for breaking God's law, and fortunately the good news is, there is a God, the creator of everything, nothing will go before Him unnoticed, he will judge every man's action according to His word whether they be good, or evil (**Prov.15:3**).[12]

For those of us who are His people, God expects us to do better in a world where everybody seems to have an opinion about anything, whether they be good or evil, especially the moral negligence that increasingly going off the chart, each time the opportunity presents itself to take a stand against it we succumb, and we give way to immorality in our lives, we forfeit the blessings of God for a brief time of pleasure.

Sadly, to say that, we oftentimes neglect our responsibility as Christians to shine the light of the gospel of Jesus Christ, in engaging ourselves in many things that are morally questionable of this world, things like sexual sins such as: fornication, adultery, masturbation, pornography, and perhaps some other perverted sexual activities that are seriously critical both on a personal level, and collectively. In an effort of bringing the light of the gospel to a world, that every human being desperately needs, every child of God ought to know and memorize these following verses "For this is the will of God, even your sanctification that ye should abstain from fornication; that everyone of you should know how to possess his vessel in sanctification and honour; not in lust of concupiscence, even as the gentiles which know not God" **I Thess. 4:3-5.**[13]

These kinds of activities ought not to be so among us Christians, we ought to be rather vessels that God can use. As the matter of fact, God wants to use you to witness to those who are rejecting His love to bring them to Him, but if your life be consistently reflected the works of the world, God will have no choice except to dispose of you, because He will not accept you to be a stumbling block for His work, He says "Ye are the salt of the earth but, if the salt have lost his savour, wherewith shall it be salted? It is thenceforth good for nothing but to be cast out, and to be trodden under foot of men. Ye are the light of the world. A city that is set on a hill cannot be hid. Neither do men light a candle, and put it under bushel, but on a candlestick; and it giveth light unto all that are in the house. Let your light so shine before men, that they may see your good works, and glorify your Father which is in heaven" (**Matt. 5:13-16**).[14]

So, you see friend, the manner of which we ought to conduct ourselves within this world, should be the exact way, that is being spoken of, in these previous verses that I quoted from the book of **Mathew**. The fact of the matter is, we can never be used of God if secretly, or openly our lives do not mirror these verses from the book of **Matthew**. Our Father in heaven can never be glorified, and therefore, because of our way of life in this world that God calls us to be separated from, there will be a downturn of morality unprecedented which we can see it, but unfortunately, we won't be able to do anything about it, because we are also the cause of it alongside with those who are not His children.

As you are looking at these assessments, I do truly believe that for the most part, we Christian are the cause of many troubles, sufferings, and pain that every human being faces in this world, because we are disobedient to God's word, and surely, we do not love God the way we ought to. Jesus said "If ye love me, keep my commandments" (**John 14:15**). These words are in accordance with God's will for our lives, so that we can be effective in His kingdom to help move those from the kingdom of darkness into the kingdom of light.[15]

The bottom line here is this: the necessity for those who have perhaps any kind of view of God, regardless the obvious of the work of the creation from His part, to come to God by the love He is shown through the shedding blood of Jesus Christ on the cross of Calvary, can never be strongly appreciated, if God's people are not right with Him. The area, I think is mostly under constant attack for a believer, is the one that questions his, or either her integrity to keep a pure, and clean sexual lifestyle within a world that produces greatly sexual perversions at all time.

It has been before the time of the flood that God saw to it that He would destroy the whole world, because of this particular sin that was out of control, even to the point there were giants upon the face of the earth which were considered to be fallen angels, maybe they were, or maybe they weren't, But in any case, those giants were sexually engaged with the daughters of men, and they bear children for them which also became giants, and so their imagination of the thoughts of their hearts were only evil continually before God, and for this cause God made a way of salvation which He had to allow a man by the name of Noah to build an ark which only his family had been spared, and all the animals that were on board following the one hundred and twenty years that Noah had to warn them about God's judgment for this kind of sin (**Gen. 6:1-7; Jude 6**).[16]

Moreover, God also later had to destroy two big cities, Sodom and Gomorrah, because of sexual perversion that was prevalent in those days. Only Lot and his family were spared from God's judgment upon those two cities. Is God going to do it again? I don't know, He may very well be, but I do know this; it is always a dangerous place to be before God when being disobedient to His word, but it is as well as a safe place to be when being obedient to His word. As we are dealing with this segment "The purpose of Sex" I hope and pray that your heart has been touched, and caused you to change, in going in the same direction of being obedient to God right where you are, so that you can be spared also from His judgment just like Noah and his family, and as well as Lot and his family (**Gen. 19:1, 24-25**).[17]

IT IS A GIFT FOR BOTH OF YOU

I am convinced, and I am also 100% sure that if we were to survey every single human being on the face of the earth, by asking everyone of them to name one thing only, that has been given to them for which they were thankful for. Without a doubt everybody with no exception including you, would name one thing, if not more than one thing they have been received for which they were thankful for. If we were to speculate, one might say as a little girl my mom gave me a doll, another would say I remember my dad gave me a dollar, my very first dollar that I ever got, and other might also say they have been abandoned an uncle, or an aunt gave a hand to them, and ever since they have a life to be thankful for, because of that uncle, and because of that aunt.

Well when you think of the issue of giving, I think there is not a single person that can truly say, he or she has nothing to be thankful for. Think about Christmases, about birthdays, anniversaries, and graduations, these are all moments where a lot of gifts are given, which allow a lot of people to receive them, and even those who expect a child, friends, and love ones organize baby showers just to give gifts, and so much more such as: wedding showers, and even during the times of sorrow, gifts are given for funeral, and so forth.

In fact, if you do not get it yet, because you can think about not so long ago the last time you said, "Thank you". It may not have been much, but you were thankful anyway for whatever it was you received. Thank you is always an expression of gratitude toward somebody, or something that was given. If you say thank you, it means you have received; something has been given to you.

I am sure at this point you get the picture, if not let me introduce you to the one that is the greatest giver of all, the ultimate gifts giver throughout all generations. He is God Almighty. After He had created the universe, He created mankind, and He gave everything to mankind to enjoy freely, He gave us the breath of life, the air to breath, the sun, the moon, the stars, He gave us knowledge, and wisdom to understand the things that He gave to us.

Finally, among of other things, God gave us His only begotten Son Jesus Christ as a gift that purchased our salvation in offering Him as the ultimate sacrifice, the only one that could satisfy God's wrath because of man's sin on the cross of Calvary. The Bible says: "For God so loved the world, that He gave His only begotten Son, that whosoever believeth in Him should not perish, but have everlasting life" (**John 3:16**). Furthermore, God not only wanted to give us His Son for our salvation, but also, He is still giving us everything because He loves us a lot, He says "He that spared not His Own Son, but delivered Him up for us all, how shall He not with Him also freely give us all things?" (**Rom.8:32**). So, you see friend that God ever since the creation began, God was in the business of giving for which He could demonstrate to us His real love even though we were yet sinners.[1]

With all these things in mind we know that God has given to us, they have been freely given to us to enjoy with no condition whatsoever even the most precious gift of salvation was also freely given to us. However, because we are dealing with gift giving as it relates to the subject at hand "It is a gift for both of you" precisely regarding sexual relation, this gift, to the exception of all other gifts that God has given to us, is the only gift that God chooses to give to mankind with a <u>condition, so that we can be right with Him as we receive it from Him.</u> If somehow anybody unwraps this gift without following through with the condition given, such action from his part puts him in direct violation to the law given for this gift, specifically, and transgresses against God Almighty that gives the law. The condition, that I am referring to, is none other than "Marriage relationship". It is only the sole platform that God allows precisely a man and a woman to engage in a sexual relationship until death due them apart, which is also their expiration date. It is not a means for two people of the opposite sexes to recreate just for the fun of it, although it may be true for those who are married.

If you can recall, I have been pondering on the basic teaching of two individuals of opposite sexes to be involved in a sexual way only through the marriage relationship throughout this entire book. In fact, the main purpose of writing this book is to bring this teaching, and to resonate it loud enough until it sinks in to the very core of our being which it will cause us to apply it each time we face it, whether before marriage, or during marriage to honor God always who gave us this gift. You know as well as I do, that if a gift is wrapped with your name on it, no one should dare to unwrap it, because of your name written on it, which also gives the authority only to you to receive it without hesitation. If besides you, somebody dares to unwrap the gift, this individual will be trespassing against, not only the person who wishes to give you the gift, but to you the recipient as well. For this cause, that is the reason why, it is always important to intentionally address the gift to the one that should receive it. No one, should in any case, steal somebody else's gift, because the whole purpose, of giving gifts in general, is the meaning for which this kind of gift, for this person specifically with the name written on it, is given.

Let me illustrate this subject "It is a gift for both of you" in the story of Abraham and Sarah his wife from the book of **Genesis chapters 15, 16, 17, 18, and 21**. It is in fact a story that basically portrays the lives of two individuals that have been married for so long and never had children of their own. They were both stricken in age, in other word; it was already past time for them to have children naturally. They were Abraham and his wife Sarah, they have been promised a child by God from which God will make of him a nation, which eventually also through this child the Messiah will come to fulfill God's promise to save the world from sin.[2]

For God to accomplish His promise to this couple regarding the need not having children, and eventually to bring forth the Messiah to the world, God is going to walk them through series of twists and turns to teach a few lessons along the way which can also be beneficial to us today. God told Abram, before He changed his name to Abraham that He (God) was His exceeding great reward in a vision (**Gen. 15:1**). Abram said to God "What wilt thou give me?" Here is the word "**give**" associating with gift, which in this case, refers to a child in the context of marriage relationship (**Gen. 15:2**).[3] Not only that, God promised Abram that He would give his seed through his natural way, not otherwise his servant's, because this promise was for an eternal covenant with God, which could not be changed, or deviate even though the world was trying to infiltrate in the plan of God, when Sarai, Abram's wife, gave her maidservant to her husband in a sexual way, in other word allowed him to commit adultery which he did, and brought forth a child as a result of it (**Gen. 16:1**).[4]

In fact, God did not honor Abram sudden move to go after his wife maidservant Hagar to have a child by her, because this move was purely worldly, and fundamentally devilish just to default God's plan of salvation for mankind. God would not use an adulterous child to carry out His plan after being specifically clear regarding His plan of what He would do.

After this instance, God would come to reaffirm His promise to Abram by changing his name to Abraham meaning the "father of many nations". By the way, it is interesting that God mentioned "The father of many nations" instead of a nation because the fact of the matter is, in God's eyes He saw the people of the world that He would allow His only begotten Son to come to die for their sins. It is through this child, Abraham's child that the ultimate sacrifice would be made possible, which would be illustrated through Abraham only begotten son (**Gen.17:1-5; Heb. 11:17**).[5]

Now God, in His wisdom would establish an unprecedented ritual, which would give a sign to Abraham, and the rest of the world after him, that this was Him doing it. Whenever they would see this sign, it would be a reminder that God had made, and sealed a covenant with Abraham forever. It was that Abraham would have circumcised himself and all other men in his household beginning from the age of eight days old, and so forth (**Gen.17:9-14**).[6]

Moreover, Sarai name would be changed also to Sarah, because of the promise since she was in fact too old to have children. And because of that, she would be sexually engaged once again with her husband Abraham to produce a child of their own under the umbrella of the covenant made to them by God, even though they seemed physically incapable to be involved as such. God will enable them to be sexually active one more time as a couple, to work this miracle out as if they were rejuvenated (**Gen. 18:10**).[7] Following that, just for Sarah to have a child at her age, God would bypass the menopausal period in her life that was already kicked in, so that there would be anything stopping her to receive God's favor to have a child at ninety years of age (**Gen. 18:11**).[8]

It was not too big of a deal, or even too difficult for God to do for them, because they were obedient to God. Besides what would appear to be a problem in the process of bringing a child into this world of their own, God took care of it, not only that, the situation with Hagar's son that would seem to be an interference of the world with God's promise to them, God also took care of it by sending Hagar and her son Ishmael away, so God's plan can accomplish fully as He intended (**Gen. 21:1-14**).[9]

In perspective, we've noticed from this segment that in fact nothing absolutely nothing is impossible with God, if you and I are obedient to His word. The understanding of giving a gift, within the context of marriage relationship from God, and receive it obediently within the same context, would result of having a child in old age in the case of Abraham and Sarah, even though naturally it was impossible to them.

"It is a gift for both of you" is not a deserving gift for anyone to brag about, but it is a blessing that God gives automatically to those who come together as couples in marriage relationship as a means to enter into a covenant relationship with God Almighty who created them, also with the family of both parties represented at the moment, because God said "What therefore God had joined together, let no man put asunder" **Matt. 19:6**.[10] It is through this act that the covenant is sealed within the context of marriage relationship with God, because when it is applied that way. It is in effect a way to say yes to God's way since He was the one who instituted marriage relationship to carry out His will, just like Jesus said "Our Father which art in heaven, hallowed be thy name. Thy kingdom come, thy will be done in earth, as it is in heaven" **Matt. 6:9-10**. That's what it is all about, that the will of God be done here in earth the same as it is in heaven.[11]

Perhaps you may be asking why this subject is of importance to you. This subject is of importance to you and for everyone for that matter, for three simple reasons:

1.   It is a gift two people of the opposite sexes to receive in marriage relationship only.

The fact of the matter is, one cannot engage in a sexual relationship with himself, or herself. It is only happening between two people of the opposite sexes, that's why God said: "In the image of God created him, male and female created He them" **(Gen. 1:27)**.[12] It is actually a gift that is for everybody, and not for everybody at the same time, the reason for it is this; if anyone chooses to be married, then automatically this gift is given, but if this individual chooses not to be married, then automatically there is no gift. So, whatever happens with the individual that chooses not to be married after that, regarding sexual relation, will be in violation with God's law. This gift particularly opens the door to God's blessing of children, not only that, it gives the opportunity for parents to inculcate God's law in their mind as they are becoming older, so that they also can know God's law to continue on with the legacy to other generations after them **(Deut. 6:1-10)**.[13] And as a result of two people of the opposite sexes receiving this gift obediently, they in turn will experience their children to be obedient to them as well with no hassle from their part to oblige them to do that according to (**Eph. 6:1-3**).[14] And on top of all that, we just said, because they received this gift obediently all the way to marriage relationship, in other word, the gift has been unwrapped only in their marriage relationship, they will be spared from any sexual transmitted diseases, or any other perverted sexual sins that the devil could throw at them, because God's hands are upon them until the end, and He also says in His word "The angel of the Lord encampeth round about them that fear Him, and delivereth them" (**Ps. 34:7**).[15]

2. It is a gift that was given for the husband to emulate Christ's relationship with His church to be for his wife (Husband).

    In the book of Ephesians, the Bible says according to verse twenty-five "Husbands, love your wives, even as Christ also loved the church, and He gave Himself for it". This command from God to the husbands, which by the way, husband is a title given to a man that is married to a woman, exactly portrays from the book of **Genesis 2:24**, is a call upon the husbands, because of the fact, they have an example to follow which they cannot duplicate, or represent in any form, but simply they ought to emulate Jesus Christ. But why emulate, why not represent, or reflect? It is to emulate because according to **Eph. 5:25**, in the middle of the verse, it says: "Even as". These two little words can be rendered also "Just as Christ also loved the church and gave Himself for it". In other word, a husband is to love, not only his wife, but also to give himself for her. We all know that it is impossible for a husband to love his wife to the point of giving himself in death for his wife. I do believe that Christ's love-work for the church is threefold, which are the past, the present, and the future. In considering these entire threefold works, what can a husband do to represent Christ, or any other verbs that can be used for him in relationship with his wife in the same plain field level with Christ and the church? I would rather suggest the verb "Emulate" because it has the idea as a husband to allow Jesus to be the husband he ought to be for his wife as he is keeping his eyes on Jesus, because He alone can love your wife through you as He would for His church.

Besides, Jesus could only number one: because of love, give Himself to redeem His church, a husband could not do that for his wife. Number two: in His love, He is sanctifying His church; a husband is incapable to do that for his wife. Number three: because of His work, sacrifice, and labor of love, He will present His church to Himself in flawless perfection, that's the reward; a husband would not be able to do that, no matter how great his sacrifice may be. It is only when a husband can allow Christ's love to manifest in him that is when he can love his wife.

Therefore, to reflect, or represent, can be done perhaps only on the level of communication in words, but in practical level he is to emulate Christ in allowing Him to be for the wife in the relationship, the husband he ought to be for her always. As a husband, he is not going to be a redeemer for his wife, but Christ can. He is not able to continually sanctify his wife, but Christ is. And finally, he does not have the power to present his wife to himself in flawless perfection, but Christ does. And so, this gift, of sexual relation between two opposite sexes, gives the opportunity of a blessed life, where Christ is the center of the relationship, because it was done in the right fashion. What a privilege that is for all of us to be blessed by God in such a way! A privilege that is so rare among the sexes considering the blatant sexual exposure in disrespect of God's law everywhere. Who wouldn't want to be touched by God? The possibility is endless, if only we learn to obey God's law.

3. It is a gift that allows a couple to manifest God's kingdom in their lives.

Normally, when two people are getting married male and female in our day, they too would make their decision on their own, and almost many times when they are ready to finalize the details of what they want to do, that's when they sort of inviting their parents in to what they plan on doing about whom they wish to spend their lives with. Family and love ones, oftentimes too excited for the big news, would come together to socially coordinate the event according to their cultures, and family tradition, and so forth, so that the big day can be a memorable one in the eyes of everyone present on that day. Unfortunately, for the most part, that's all it is because prior to the big day, both sets of family, that would allow their kids to be joined in marriage, had no opportunity to sit together, and get to know each family of every side to which after a while, they would determine whether, or not they would join each other's family in marriage.

Furthermore, it usually happens that the purpose of a couple joining in marriage is because of an unexpected pregnancy. This crazy solution to be brought among the sexes, after being foolishly sexually engaged, is often occurs among the Christian circle, for the fact, that they want to show the world they are not in the habit of tolerating sin, that's what they would offer (Marriage) to avoid any further embarrassment. Suffice it to say, by doing what they are doing to prevent more damages to their testimony as Christians, or perhaps as respectable people in the community, would lead them to more troubles unless they cease their drama, resolve among themselves to live their lives inwardly and outwardly according to God's living standard, His word.

And that's what happened in the old days, marriage

was not a social business, it was an intricate part that was vitally important in everyone's life to define what the next step would be spiritually. Therefore, it was totally up to the parents to lead their children into this important journey they were to undertake for the rest of their lives. It was not a question that the kids could make up their own mind regarding this issue of marriage, and it was to be done by order of the child in the family. A younger sister would not get married before the older sister would, or a younger brother before the older, and so forth. This sort of custom, or tradition if you will, was in fact God's way of preparing His people to be involved in His kingdom on earth as He would guard them with His directives, in enabling them to do that which He commanded them, to be set apart for His exceptional use (**Gen.29: 16- 35**). Back in those days, it was not like it is today, that a young lady would go out to fornicate with her boyfriend, and after that expected to get married. No, it wasn't so, if she was found not a virgin, she would probably get killed, or send back to her parents which she would never get married because of the shame she brought to her family in the land (**Gen. 34**).

In accordance with this line of thinking, I am going to share with you a story from the Bible, which I think will be helpful to you to understand this gift that God has given to us mankind clearly from His perspective as an eternal God. And I also believe this story can help many of you unmarried men and women who perhaps have been involved in some sexual relations in the past, or perhaps are not involved at all, but wish to be involved some day in the right context. There are also many parents who perhaps are not following God's way of bringing up their children whom their children may, or may not have been sexually active, so they are so desperate for a change, or a move of God in their favor. The story is the one that walks us through the way God allowed Abraham to find a bride for his son Isaac, the promised one. The story is found in **Genesis 24.**

Abraham, Isaac's father, is very cautious about the woman whom is going to marry his son, the promised one. For this reason, he is giving his servant some words of advice by which he would know the appointed one for his master's son. One of the words of caution that he gave him was, he would not take one of the Canaanites daughters **(Gen.24:3)**.[16] Understand the context of this passage of Scripture, that Abraham would send his servant back to his kindred, in search for a virgin woman for his son Isaac to marry. One of the reasons that he warned him that way was, the Canaanites daughters did not know the true living God (Jehovah). They only knew other gods, many of them which were indeed abomination before God. The Bible teaches us that we should not have other gods before Jehovah God **(Ex. 20:3)**. This warning against other gods of the world is a principle that applies to all of us in to enter God's perfect will for all our lives human beings.[17]

Abraham also underscores the importance of this woman who will be his son's wife to have this clear foundation willingly to follow, which would be tremendously helpful for his son marriage relationship **(Gen.24:8)**. This ought to be every man's desire to find in every woman's heart the willingness to follow her husband.[18] It is a principle that is vitally important for the health of a marriage relationship, because God commands it to be, so for wives to submit to their own husbands **(Eph. 5:22; Col. 3:18).** Besides, this principle enables God to work through the couple in the relationship, in influencing them to follow God's way, and others that are not part of the family, to experience a little taste of His divine blessing. This principle in this context is not a suggestion for some, and for others, it is a command to adhere to. It is a collective package of God's wonderful plan for those who wish to marry, because it would be hypocritical and unfair to want God's gift of sexual relation within the context of marriage relationship, and at the same time to reject His command which is the very essence of the relationship. Make no mistakes, at any given moment one can submit to do something because of duress, or other form of pressure, but here it is to submit willingly to follow, that's God's way.[18]

In addition, to be willing to follow, Abraham requested to his servant that the woman had to be a virgin, so that she could marry his son Isaac (**Vs. 16**). You see, Abraham knew the value of the covenant that God made with him regarding the promised child. He needed to safeguard this child in every way of his life, and even when he was about to make a lifetime commitment such as marriage. It was important to Abraham to do, because primarily, that's what God wanted him to do, in focusing to His word, and applying it as it was prescribed, so that God's will would be done in their lives according to that which He had promised. The same it is important to us to understand that God's way should always prevail in our lives. His word should be the blueprint upon which we live our lives, especially with things that relate to sexual relationship, such as marriage, having children, and so forth.[20] Abraham's servant wanted to be certain before he was to find a woman for his master's son. He did not rely on his personal intuition, or knowledge to execute the mission he had; he stopped and offered a twofold prayer to God, which was firstly an intercessory prayer on behalf of his master Abraham for God's kindness upon him. Secondly, he offered a specific detailed prayer, which enabled not only him to make the choice, but also it will give him the woman for his master's son to go home with (**Gen. 24:12-14**).[21]

Here is in this passage of scriptures a good example to follow in our lives, when it comes to human romantic relationship, to be sure that it is in fact God's will to consider marrying to start a family. Because the fact of the matter is, relationship begins with God, and continues with God. If begin a life otherwise, chances are the benefits, and the promises that God offers through His word may not in no wise available for those of us who choose not to have a romantic relationship according to His word (**Matt. 7:24-25**).[22]

Furthermore, it was customary that parents of both sides before they exercised the directives of God Almighty, which is "Therefore shall a man leave his father and his mother and shall cleave unto his wife; and they shall be one flesh" (**Gen. 2:24**). They would administer to their children what we call "Parental blessing" which is part of the process of letting go of their children to begin their own life as they about to become one flesh.

It is also a way to know that as parents, they are in this union together as support to their children's union, both physically, and spiritually[23]. In fact, it has been for generations the ritual upon which they built their lives as they carried out God's way throughout all their generations, in fulfilling their purposes with love and equity, before God and men. It has been also the awesome privilege to do so, because they knew that's what God wanted them to do, also they would wholeheartedly pass on these values to their children, which in turn would live their lives as such, and would also pass on those values to their children for a perpetual devotion. Later, both Isaac and Jacob blessed their children consecutively as they come to the end of their lives, so that the blessings they had received from their fathers could continue to touch their offspring, even though they departed from this world (**Heb. 11:20-21**).[24]

It is with the same interest that they had, in their days, to follow God's way in everything in all the aspects of their lives, that we people of this twenty-first century generation, and other generations to come, should embrace God's way of life wholeheartedly as they did especially in romantic relationship area, so that we can be blessed as they were in health, wealth, longevity of life, and so forth. God's love will be made manifest among us, His name will be lifted, not only in words, but also in our action toward each other, and we will have the power to trample under feet the enemy that is out to destroy our lives, our relationship with each other, our relationship with God our creator, and finally to defeat the deeds of the enemy always in all aspects of our lives.

As you can see, when Rebekah's parents were ready to send her away, they did not push her away as if she did not have anything to say. Besides, she was the one who would have, not only to go, but to live with somebody she was yet to meet for the rest of her life. Other inputs in marrying Isaac, the husband to be, was as much important as her parents' in making the decision to begin a romantic relationship with a potential life partner. Yes, her parents had to employ wisdom in seeking God's will for her life as to whom she would be marrying, but at the same time she was to know whether this was her heart's desire, or not to leave her parents' home to go and live with another family in marriage relationship. Rebekah's father came consulting with her to find out where her heart was in the issue at hand regarding the proposal offered by Abraham's servant in regard of her becoming the bride that he was looking for (**Gen. 24:57-59**).[25]

Needless to say, many times the marriages of our day fail even before they begin, because there was not a concerting effort among the families, the bride and the groom to be sure about the means they would exercise with which they would bring these two in marriage relationship, and their families for an eternal covenant, both before God and before men. We all ought to learn from Isaac and Rebekah's union, so that we can know for sure that we have done it the right way with no regrets. Meanwhile Isaac did his part in seeking God while he hopefully waited to find a wonderful bride, a life partner (**Gen. 24:63**).[26]

Isaac was made aware of his father's servant report concerning the mission he had on his behalf. He was pleased that everything turned out great, because God's hand was upon the entire process up to that point, and he also brought Rebekah to his mother's tent in memory of her as if he was looking for her blessing. Isaac wedded Rebekah, and he knew her sexually, that was perfect.

The point that I was trying to make with the story of Isaac and Rebekah's union was that "The blessing of the Lord, it maketh rich, and He addeth no sorrow with it" (**Prov. 10:22**). Two people came to be together as one, did not defile themselves sexually, and were able to remain virgin until they tied the knot in marriage relationship, just as the Lord intended it for them. They did not have to go through series of hardship because of violation of God's law, nor did they have to enter the marriage forcefully because of unwanted pregnancy, or other reasons. They just simply loved God, followed their parents' guidance, which brought them together in perfect harmony. They did not have to look back to regret their mistakes, but rather to count their blessings as they continued to seek God's will for their lives as one, in sickness, in health, for riches until death due them apart. They lived happily ever after because of their obedience to God's law, and because of their willingness to uphold God's way for the rest of their lives just like their parents did.[27]

It is not impossible for us people of this present time to conduct our lives in such a way to please God. We just need to resolve to say, enough is enough, we will make sure to do what it takes to maintain a healthy life, both physically and spiritually, as we will pursue God's way to love Him and honor Him in everything we say and do just like Joshua had said "And if seem evil unto you to serve the Lord, choose you this day whom ye will serve _____ but as for me and my house, we will serve the Lord" (**Joshua 24:15**). This ought to be every man and every woman heart desire to seek after, so that our lives will not be in danger, and certainly we will have a bright future with benefits.[28]

AFTER WORDS

The product of this book had been brought to you intentionally to press upon your heart the need to retaliate against the pluralistic world view of morality of this present world. In all sincerity, we all can attest that the moral state of our world, or rather the moral condition of our being as individual precisely, has been damaged ever since we abandoned the principle of absolute truth, and the supreme authority that should guide us to it, in all the aspects of our lives whether it be family, government, school, relationship, business, religion, etc. The beginning of our moral decline unfortunately began with the first family of humans, where they rejected God's truth over a relative truth that was somehow more intriguing to them, but this cannot be as today the excuse with which to justify the moral condition of our being as individual, or as human race collectively. We have had to be better to change the world than it was in the 80's, and the 90's, the time when H.I.V Aids was prevalent because of inappropriate sexual conducts among the sexes, also when teen pregnancies were at its high, it was like an epidemic of the worse kind, because everywhere you turned kids were having babies prematurely.

Today, it seems that there is no way to stop the moral decline of our world, so that we can protect ourselves, and the ones we love. Sexual perversion of all sorts is widely practiced in the open. We've come from neglecting our responsibility of rejecting the inappropriate sexual conducts such as: fornication which is having sex before marriage, adultery which is having sex with somebody other than our spouse to embrace, or to tolerate the worse kind of sexual perversion such as: homosexuality, lesbianism, bestiality, swapping partners, transvestites, and much more to name a few. On top of that, we have arrived at a point of equalizing the union of two men and two women in marriage, as the same marriage relationship between a man and a woman as God instituted it in the first place. We have decided once again to abandon God's truth concerning this marriage relationship, to accept another relativism truth to make marriage relationship whatever else we want it to be. Who knows, some day we might see humans marry their pets, or perhaps some other stupid relationship they would come with, may God have mercy on us!

God some time ago in two separate occasions had demonstrated His fury against such inappropriate behaviors, and the wickedness of man for not willing to obey His word. These two instances were first, the universal flood God brought upon the earth during the time of Noah and his family. Second, the extermination of Sodom and Gomorrah, God did it because they wickedly abandoned God's way, and for specifically engaging in immoral sexual lifestyle. For that, God had to destroy these two cities, and yet at the same time protected Lot and his family, Abraham's nephew.

Now you have the facts of what happened to those who engaged in the manner of which that displeased God in the past. What makes you think that God would not take the same measure, or even a more drastic one, that is worse than the ones before, in these two instances mentioned earlier against us? The truth of the matter is, there is no certainty of what God would do against those who stand in opposition to Him at any time. One thing that is certain, that God will always deal with the sin, and punish the sinner, you just need to make sure you don't fall under the hand of God.

I guess the lesson we all need to learn from this book is this: God loves everyone of us, He does not want any of us to perish, but to have everlasting life through His Son Jesus Christ, but if any of us stand in rebellion before Him concerning His word, His absolute truth, He will destroy you, there is no doubt.

This book is an effort from my part as an author to help you realize the gravity of violating God's law, and at the same time to understand that you still have a chance to have a pure life, and a close relationship with God Almighty the creator, and with people around you in the proper context of human, or romantic relationship. Remember, because we are all part of humanity, it means that we are also the work of God's hand in His creation, His goal has always been for you and me to live purely, and happily before Him, so that we can make up a people that He has in mind for His pleasure before the world began.

At this time, as you come to finish reading the book, I encourage you to make up your mind in dealing with the issues we discussed in this book "Why guilt …. After sex in a world of perfect perversion?" whether you have been educated about the issues, or perhaps you have been touched, or moved to stand by morality once again, in helping to protect humanity from destroying lives with myriad of sexual perversions, and immoralities in our midst. I hope and trust that this book has done a work in your life as you would stand with me to fight the doctrine of relativism of a pluralistic mindset in this world, to uphold God's truth as the banner of righteousness, and as our light to guide us through the paths of this life, so that we can fulfill God's purpose, and our destiny within it.

May we all be agents of righteousness throughout our lives, to put down evil in our midst, as we keep our eyes on Jesus the author and the finisher of our faith until, the day of our complete redemption from this world to rejoice with Him forever! Until then, may He grant us grace and mercy, as we lovingly walk humbly before Him according to His word!

NOTES AND BIBLIOGRAPHY

CHAPTER ONE
THE SEXUALITY IS REVEALED

1 Male bamboo or PVC pipe, fishing basket, and others: old fashion custom during the time of the colony in the Caribbean countries such as: Hispaniola, Cuba, Jamaica, Belize, Martinique, etc
2 Ibid
3 A person or thing regarded as an exact copy of another. Oxford American dictionary and thesaurus second edition, 2009 page, 229
4 Ibid, page1413
5 The Holy Bible the authorized King James version New York Oxford University Press, edited by Rev. C.I. Scofield, D.D. Hebrews 9:27 page, 1299
6 Ibid, page,623
7 Ibid, page, 1215
8 Ibid, pages, 8 and 1025

IT IS GOOD TO HAVE SEX

1 Oxford American dictionary and thesaurus second edition, 2009 page,
2 Ibid, pages, 1096 – 1195

THE MINDSET OF SEX IN TODAY'S WORLD

1 Campos, David Santa Barbara, California 2002. "Sex, youth, and sex education" a reference handbook. Page, 168
2 Ibid, page, 168

3   Ibid, pages, 168 -69
4   Ibid, page, 22
5   Ibid, page, 22
6   Ibid, page, 22

CHAPTER TWO
WHAT IS SEX TO YOU?

1   To gain territories, another type of pleasure to enjoy, a priceless gift, one of the marital fulfillments, a means of reproduction: Each one is testimonial of individuals who think sex is as such.

IT IS NOT GOOD TO HAVE SEX

1   Liberating; testimony from co-worker, 2008
2   Fulfilling: testimony of people from different walks of life interviewed for the book "Why guilt ... after sex" 2009-2010
3   Power, Ibid
4   Gain territories, Ibid
5   Trap, Ibid
6   Weapon, Ibid
7   Tool, Ibid
8   Useful product in the wrong hands, Ibid
9   Solid link, Ibid
10   Sex is whatever is plant, Ibid
11   Form of payment, Ibid
12   Sex is strictly business, Ibid
13   Another type of pleasure to enjoy, Ibid
14   Priceless gift, Ibid
15   Another level of commitment, Ibid
16   One of the marital fulfillments, Ibid
17   A means of reproduction, Ibid
18   The way by which two become one, Ibid
19   The door by which life begins, Ibid
20   An opportunity to live or to die, Ibid
21   A way to know somebody in a different level, Ibid
22   Alexander the great, ruler of Macedonia

23   The Holy Bible the authorized King James version, New York University Press, edited by C.I. Scofield D.D. Judges 21:25, page, 314

24   Ibid, page, 1247

IT IS NOT GOOD TO HAVE SEX

1   The Holy Bible the authorized King James version, New York University Press, edited by C.I. Scofield D.D. Genesis 2:24, page 8

THE DANGER IS YET TO DISCOVER

1   OLR Research Report: 2003-R-0376 Statutory Rape Laws byState: by Sandra norman Eady, chief attorney, Christopher Reinhart, associate attorney, Peter Martino, research fellow, April 14, 2003

2   The 2011 Florida Statutes. Title XLVI crimes, chapter 794 sexual battery, 794.0115. Dangerous sexual feleny offender; mandatory sentencing. Online Sunshine

3   Ibid,

SEX AND LOVE

1   Deadly virus H.I.V.

2   Results of the H.I.V. virus such as: cold, fever, airborne diseases

3   Wikipedia websites. United States Declaration of Independence

4   The Holy Bible the authorized King James version, New York University Press, edited by C.I. Scofield D.D. pages, 1004, 1080

5   Go after what you want no matter what. Author unknown

6   The Holy Bible the authorized King James Version, New York University Press, edited by C.I. Scofield D.D. page, 1247

7   To fornicate or to sodomite

8   The Holy Bible the authorized King James Version, New York University Press, edited by C.I. Scofield D.D. page, 1223-24

9   Ibid, page, 8

CAN EVERYONE BE SEXUALLY INVOLVED?

1   The Holy Bible, the authorized King James Version, New York University Press, edited by Rev. C.I. Scofield D.D. page, 698
2   Viagra, Cialis, and others, TV commercials, author unknown
3   Mango trees planted for a period of 5 and 6 years
4   The Holy Bible, the authorized King James Version, New York University Press, edited by Rev. C.I. Scofield D.D. page, 8
5   Ibid, page, 1247

I DON'T LOVE YOU I AM IN IT JUST FOR THE MONEY

1   Traditional romantic courtship from the countries of the Caribbean.
2   Musical groups called "Troubadours" (Caribbean, Hispaniola)
3   The child abandonment law (Caribbean, Hispaniola)
4   The trend of the 30's, and 40's: "I don't love you …"
5   The 2008-2009 ABC's TV series "Bachelor and Bachelorette"

THE SEX FACTOR

1   Evelyn, Lerman "Safer sex the new morality" page, 32
2   Ibid
3   Ibid, page 33
4   The Holy Bible, the authorized King James version, New York University Press, edited by Rev. C.I. Scofield, D.D. page 8
5   Evelyn, Lerman "Safer sex the new morality" pages, 74-75
6   Ibid

THE PERVERSION OF SEX

1   The Holy Bible the authorized King James Version, New York University Press, edited by Rev. C.I. Scofield D.D. pages, 151, 1192
2   Ralph, Button "The wrath of God revealed" sermon, and The Holy Bible the authorized King James Version, New York University Press, edited by C.S. Scofield D.D. pages, 151, and 1192
3   Ibid, page, 667
4   Ibid, pages, 1233, 1013

5   M. Larue, Janet CWA websites internet article "Pornography and Figures" dated August 10, 2010

THE MONEY MAKING, THE INDUSTRY BUILT BY SEX

1   The Holy Bible the authorized King James Version, New York University Press, edited by Rev. C.I. Scofield D.D. page, 9
2   Old saying during the time of the colony. Author unknown
3   Ibid,
4   M. Larue, Janet CWA websites internet article "Pornography and Figures" dated August 10, 2010
5   The Holy Bible the authorized King James Version, New York University Press, edited by Rev. C.I. Scofield D.D. page, 682
6   Ibid, page, 683
7   M. Larue, Janet CWA websites internet article "Pornography and Figures" dated August 10, 2010
8   The Holy Bible the authorized King James Version, New York University Press, edited by Rev. C.I. Scofield D.D. page 682
9   Ibid, page, 1277
10 Ibid, pages, 1262-63
11 Ibid, page, 1309
12 Ibid, page1269

THE BEAUTY OF SEX

1   The Holy Bible the authorized King James Version, New York University Press, edited by Rev. C.I. Scofield D.D. page, 8
2   Ibid,
3   Ibid,
4   Ibid, pages 8-9
5   Ibid, page 5
6   Ibid, pages 3, 5, 6
7   Ibid,
8   Ibid, page, 1002
9   Ibid, pages, 24-25
10 Ibid, pages, 8, 1314, 1254-55, 1265, 223-24
11 Ibid, pages, 1254-55
12 Ibid, page, 8

13   Ibid, pages, 8, 10
14   Ibid, page, 8
15   Ibid, pages, 5-6, 8
16   Ibid, pages, 6-7
17   Ibid, page, 683
18   Ibid,
19   Ibid, page, 314
20   Ibid, page, 683

NO MORE SEX

1   The Holy Bible the authorized King James Version, New York University
       Press, edited by Rev. C.I. Scofield D.D. Page, 243
2   Ibid, page, 55
3   Ibid, page, 1025
4   Ibid, page, 1220
5   Ibid, page,1218
6   Ibid, pages, 55-56
7   Ibid, pages, 993-4
8   Ibid, pages, 5-6
9   Ibid, page, 1202
10   "What you don't know can't hurt you" Author unknown
11   The holy Bible the authorized King James Version, New York University
       Press, edited by Rev. C.I. Scofield D.D. page, 1309
12   Ibid, page, 1199
13   Ibid, page, 55
14   Ibid, page, 1004
15   Ibid, pages, 1194, 1199
16   Ibid, page, 243
17   Ibid,
18   Ibid, page, 55
19   Ibid, page, 1034
20   Ibid, pages, 687-88
21   Ibid, page, 658
22   Ibid, page, 1304
23   Ibid, page, 1204
24   Ibid, page, 803
25   Ibid, page, 55

26 Ibid, page, 647

27 Ibid, page, 1060

28 Ibid, pages, 1114, 1252, 1262-63

29 Ibid, page, 1065,

30 Ibid, pages, 55, 243

31 Ibid, pages 682

32 Ibid, pages, 1044, 1069

33 Ibid, pages, 20, 23, 25, 1044, 1069, 1284

THE PURPOSE OF SEX

1 The Holy Bible the authorized King James Version, New York University Press, edited by Rev. C.S. Scofield D.D. page, 9

2 Ibid, page, 674

3 Ibid, page, 1025

4 Ibid, pages, 1004-5

5 Ibid, pages, 1265, 1254-55

6 Ibid, pages, 5-6

7 Ibid, pages, 694, 676

8 Slaterry, Juli "No more headaches enjoy sex and intimacy in marriage" Carol stream, Illinois Tyndale, 2009, pages, 18-19

9 The Holy Bible the authorized King James Version, New York University Press, edited by Rev. C.I. Scofield D.D. page, 672

10 Ibid, page, 673

11 Ibid, page, 673

12 Ibid, page, 682

13 Ibid, page, 1269

14 Ibid, page, 999

15 Ibid, page, 1136

16 Ibid, pages, 14, 1328

17 Ibid, pages, 28-29

IT IS A GIFT FOR BOTH OF YOU

1 The Holy Bible the authorized King James Version, New York University Press, edited by Rev. C.I. Scofield D.D. pages 1117-18, 1202

2 Ibid, pages, 24-25

3 Ibid, pages, 23-24

4   Ibid, page, 25
5   Ibid, pages, 26, 1302
6   Ibid, pages, 26-27
7   Ibid, page, 28
8   Ibid,
9   Ibid, page, 31
10 Ibid, page, 1025
11 Ibid, page, 1002
12 Ibid, page, 5
13 Ibid, pages, 223-24
14 Ibid, page, 1255
15 Ibid, page, 614
16 Ibid, page, 35
17 Ibid, page, 95
18 Ibid, page, 35
19 Ibid, pages, 1254, 1265
20 Ibid, page, 35
21 Ibid,
22 Ibid, page, 1004
23 Ibid, page, 8
24 Ibid, page, 1302
25 Ibid, page, 37
26 Ibid,
27 Ibid, page, 679
28 Ibid, page 285

GLOSSARY

PROLOGUE

Inculcate: *Verb. It is to impress in the mind, as by admonition*

Righteousness: *The act of being morally right. It is to receive from God by faith after a sinner has been declared righteous.*

Trend: *Noun. It is the tendency to go in a direction; up to date*

Social Relativism: *It is the belief that morality sexually speaking is not always the same, or physical attraction, or intimate contact between two people.*

Sexual Libertine: *It is the belief that there is no boundary in being sexually involved. It is to have a dissolute or licentious attitude in this area.*

Adhere: *It is to hold closely, as to an idea or course, to be devoted.*

Implementation: *It is to provide with implement or means; to execute.*

INTRODUCTION

Vulnerability: *The state of being vulnerable which is being defenseless or wounded.*

Lustful: *Adj. it is to have the feeling lust, lecherous, or passionate, or lewd desire.*

Veracity: *Something that is truthful, or accurate.*

Corridor (s): *It is a narrow passageway*

Welfare: *It is the state of being prosperous, or in a healthy condition.*

Vex (Ed): *It is the feeling of being angry or displeased.*

Holy Spirit: *God's name represented as the third person of the trinity.*

CHAPTER ONE
THE SEXUALITY IS REVEALED

Sexuality: *It is defined here from the creator God point of view which is the life how it was given and determined to live by God Himself beyond the gender boundary. It is not defined to suggest the practice of one sexual lifestyle in the open, but rather the actual fabric of an individual make up, the one that cannot be altered.*

Pregnancy: *Native, it is the fact that one can carry unborn young. (married)*

Male Bamboo: *It is the belief system that indicates when a married woman had never carried a baby in the old days. It was viewed as being unable to reproduce the same as it was for a male bamboo.*

P.V.C. Pipe: *It is rather being arrogant to express to a woman which is impossible to bring forth a child whether it is a medical problem or not. It is seen just like the P.V.C. pipe as being shallow inside with no substance.*

Fishing Basket: *In many places of underdeveloped countries fishing is not a sport, but a way of life. The fishing baskets are made purposely to drain water after being put in the water to only catch the fish. It is said to a woman who cannot bear a child to be as such because she cannot keep the seed that is planted inside of her.*

Barren: *Old English expression just to mean "Sterile" which a woman is incapable of producing offspring.*

Mindset: *It is the direction of one's thinking.*

Physiology: *It is the science that deals with processes of living.*

Clone (in): *It is the act to clone in growing an organism from a single cell by a sexual reproduction. To copy or to imitate closely as to produce an almost identical twin. It comes from the Greek word klÒn, twig.*

Origin: *It is a source, a beginning, ancestry.*

Nakedness: *The idea of being naked. It is the exposed of one's body without covering.*

Irrefutable: *It is impossible to refute which is to overthrow by argument, evidence or proof.*

Pretense: *A claim, it is a false profession based on a sham.*

Mimic: *It is to imitate.*

Testosterone: *It is the hormone secreted by the testicles also used medically to enhance masculinity to a transgender.*

Conception: *It is the effect of conceiving, an idea, a notion, and pregnancy.*

Steward: *A manager, a chief servant.*

Parameter: *It is in effect a variable quantity whose values depend on a special case.*

Standard: *It is a way of measuring, a basis of comparison.*

Oneness: *Unity or uniformity, the constancy in feeling or purpose.*

Virginity: *it is the fact of being virgin since birth. It is to abstain from sexual activity since birth.*

Precedence: *It is the act of going before or the right of taking a more honored position.*

IT IS GOOD TO HAVE SEX

Dogmatic: *To rigidly hold principle or doctrine.*

Premise: *It is a previous statement from which something is inferred or concluded.*

Aeronautics: *The art or the science of flying.*

Imminent: *It is likely something to occur soon, it is overhanging (danger).*

Prejudice: *It is bias, an opinion formed without adequate reasons, it is unfavorable.*

Vehemently: *It is how to show strength, intensely to a degree.*

Intact: *Whole. Complete, it is to stay uninjured.*

Diagnosis: *It is the analysis of present condition.*

Endeavor: *To work hard at something, or to exert oneself to do something.*

Propagation: *Is the fact of propagating which is to increase or enlarge.*

Authentic: *It is the ascribed authorship, the origin or duly authorized.*

Correctness: *It is the idea of rectifying, to note or to mark errors.*

Woe (s): *It is an intense unhappiness, grief, sorrow or affliction.*

Incompetence: *Adj. That which is not fit or capable; one that is inadequate to a task.*

Avalanche: *It is the sudden fall of a mass of ice or debris down the side of a mountain. It is also used metaphorically to describe the sudden invading of a group or an ideology or the propagation of a doctrine.*

CHAPTER TWO
WHAT IS SEX TO YOU?

Rupture: *It is in some instance the breach of a peace; it is also the act of breaking …*

Lust (s): *It is the intense longing for possession of something or it is the passionate or lewd desire.*

Abstinence: *N. It is the ability to self-restraint in satisfaction of appetite.*

Disintegrating: *it is the act of disintegrate which is to separate into parts or go to pieces.*

Privilege: *N. It is a special advantage enjoyed by a person.*

Responsibility: *It is the state of being responsible which can satisfy any reasonable claim, involving important work or trust.*

Accountability: *It is the fact that a person can explain, to be liable or responsible.*

Restriction: *It is the ability to restrict which is to attach limitations to, the limit of something.*

Precarious: *It is uncertain, insecure, and dangerous.*

Puberty: *It is the time, or the age of a person's life can first procreate. It is the developmental process the results in puberty, the sexual maturation.*

Ramification: *it is first a branch or subdivision, but it is also the consequence or the extended effect of an action.*

IT IS NOT GOOD TO HAVE SEX

Unwavering: *Something that is characterized by absence of fluctuation. Expl. An unwavering faith in God.*

THE DANGER IS YET TO COME

Detrimental: *Adj. having to work to the detriment of something which is in effect an injury or less or perhaps that which causes it.*

F.B.I.: *Federal Bureau of Investigation*

Statutory: *Adj. it is the condition with which defines the statute which is an ordinance or the law.*

Pornography: *From Greek word porne, prostitute, the word literally means the depiction of prostitutes, at first applied to classical drawings, such as the paintings at Pompeii.*

Predator: *it is one that preys, destroys, or devours.*

Incarceration: *It is a confining or estate of being confined such as imprisonment.*

Predicament: *It is in effect a position imposing a hard or unwelcome choice, dilemma, perplexity.*

CHAPTER THREE
SEX AND LOVE

H.I.V.: *Human immunodeficiency of virus.*

Antagonistic: *It is marked by or something is arising from opposition, hostility, or discord.*

Bias: *It is an inclination of temperament or outlook. It is also a tendency of an estimate to deviate in one direction from a true value.*

Stubbornness: *it is the quality or state of being stubborn which is in effect difficult to handle, work, or manage.*

Distinctively: *it is having a distinctive manner which is to distinguish or setting apart from others.*

Fornicate: *It is sexual act between the sexes before marriage*

Sodomite: *It is to practice the sodomy which is the homosexual proclivities of the men of the city of Sodom narrated in Gen. 19:1-11. Carnal copulation with a member of the same sex.*

Infraction: *it is the act of breaking or violating the established law for something.*

CAN EVERYONE BE SEXUALLY INVOLVED?

Modality: *The quality or the state of being modal, modal quality, attribute, or circumstance.*

Venture: *To expose to risk or hazard; it is to face or to undertake the risks or dangers of.*

Criteria: *N. pl. it is a standard on which a decision or judgment may be used.*

Consistency: *The condition … of standing together or remaining fixed in union.*

Reluctant: *Offering opposition, hesitant from or as if from dislike, doubts, fear, scruple.*

Intolerable: *Not tolerable, not capable of being borne or endured.*

Laissez faire: *it is a policy of non-interference especially a policy disallowing governmental regulation of economic affairs.*

Desolation: *The condition of being desolated, a state of ruin, dilapidation, devastation.*

I DON'T LOVE YOU I AM IN IT JUST FOR SEX

Serenade: *N. an evening song of love, it is also to entertain with a serenade.*

Troubadour (s): *It is in effect an itinerant lyric poet or singer.*

Precarious: *Uncertain, insecure.*

Solace: *It is comfort in sorrow.*

Eager: *Adj. it is having keen desire or longing, being impatient.*

Ambiance: *It is the atmosphere, the mood, the environment.*

Dogmatic: *Positive, it is adhering rigidly to a tenet.*

Ill: *Causing evil, unfriendly.*

Emphatically: *That which is done in the emphatic manner which is marked by emphasis, made prominent by stress.*

Prevalent: *Adj. it is of wide use or occurrence; widespread.*

Pertube (Ed): *Verb. To agitate, disturb greatly.*

Directive (s): *It is in fact an instruction, or a statement of policy.*

THE SEX FACTOR

Chaperon: *N. an older person, usually a married woman accompanying younger unmarried persons.*

Contraception: *N. it is a means or a method of preventing conception birth control.*

Jeopardize: *Risk, danger, imperil*

Advocacy: *It is the act of advocating which is to plead in favor of, defend in argument.*

Apparatus: *It is in effect all the equipment used for some purpose.*

Triune: *Being three in one, the unity of the trinity in the Godhead.*

Cleave: *This word has two opposite meanings. 1 Adhere, stick, cling. 2 Rend asunder, split.*

CHAPTER FOUR
THE PERVERSION OF SEX

Narcissistic: *Relating to narcissism which is over evaluation of one's own attributes or achievements or of those of one's group. Egoism, egocentrism.*

Rally: *It is to draw or call together for a common purpose; Assemble and reconstitute as a disorganized army.*

Leverage: *The action of a lever; it is the mechanical advantage it provides.*

Comply: *It is to acquiesce in another's wish, command.*

Heterosexual: *Adj. it is to manifest sexual desire toward a member of the opposite sex. A heterosexual person.*

Devilish: *Adj. like a devil which is the supreme evil spirit, Satan.*

Contemplate: *VT it is viewed or reflected upon attentively. Meditate.*

Adamant: *Adj. hard, hardhearted; unyielding.*

Component: *Adj. forming a part of, N. a constant part.*

Masturbation: *N. sexual self-gratification, to masturbate.*

Perception: *N. the act or the faculty of perceiving. Something perceived.*

Perspective: *It is the point of view, the proper relative position of objects or phenomena one perceives.*

THE MONEY MAKING THE INDUSTRY BUILT BY SEX

Transpose: *The idea of altering the position or order. It is to exchange places.*

Crude: *It is in a raw or unprepared state.*

Normalcy: *It is the state, the condition or fact of being normal which occurs naturally.*

Alleviate: *Lighten, lessen, relieve, moderate, to make easier to be endured.*

Myriad: *It is a countless number, an immense number, and indefinitely substantial number.*

Prevalence: *The quality, the fact, or condition of being prevalent which is power, it is the degree to which something (as a disease, an infective agent) is prevalent.*

Nuisance: *It is an offensive, annoying, unpleasant, or obnoxious thing or practice.*

Surreal: *It is the one that has the characteristic of surrealism which is the principles, the ideal, or practice of producing or incongruous imagery art or literature by means of unnatural juxtapositions and combinations.*

CHAPTER V
THE BEAUTY OF SEX

Covenant: *To promise solemnly by or as if by a covenant, to pledge in formal agreement.*

Prerogative: *A right attached to an office or rank to exercise a special privilege or function.*

Cleave: *To adhere firmly or closely as though evenly and securely glued.*

Debauchery: *It is an extreme indulgence in sensuality, excessive indulgence of sexual desire.*

Blatantly: *In a blatant manner which is noisy, loud or clamorous.*

Distortion: *An altering or perverting that essentially falsifies true or accurate facts or true significance.*

Promiscuous: *Consisting a heterogonous or haphazard mixture of persons or thing. Composed of all sorts and conditions.*

NO MORE SEX

Meticulously: *The quality or state of being meticulous which is marked by extreme painstaking care in the consideration or treatment of details.*

To alter: *To cause to become different in some characteristic.*

Validity: *The quality or state of being valid.*

Genuine: *having the reputed or apparent qualities or character not adulterated or cheapened.*

Courtship: *The relationship between a couple from awakening of deep interest to formal engagement.*

THE PURPOSE OF SEX

Directive: *Serving or qualified to lead, guide, or govern thought or action usually by prompting and impelling rather than by dominating*

Authenticate: *To verify the origin of, to prove the authorship of.*

Indigenous: *Not introduced directly and indirectly according to historical record of scientific analysis into a land or region or environment from the outside.*

Paramount: *Superior to all others (as in power, or position, or importance)*

Demise: *To pass by descent or bequest; transference of the sovereignty to a successor.*

Libertinism: *The quality or state of being libertine or the principle or behavior of a libertine.*

Tangible: *It is constituting or consisting of a corporeal item capable of being appraised at an actual or approximate value.*

Capitulate: *To ascent to terms arranged or proposed.*

Rampant: *It is threatening or extravagant in action bearing, or manner displaying aggression or violence.*

Hell: *A place created by God for the devil, demons, and the damned awaiting them after the judgment. It is a place of torment and misery.*

Oblivion: *it is an act of forgetting, the quality or state of being forgotten.*

Wedge: *Something (as a device, policy, or action) causing a breach or separation.*

IT IS A GIFT FOR BOTH OF YOU

Bypass: *It is a passage to o¹ne side, to make a circuit or detour around.*

Menopausal: *it is to undergo menopause which is the period of natural cessation of menstruation occurring usually between the ages of 45 and 50; also called change life.*

Intricate: *To entangle, or nicely or complexly interrelating parts, phases, patterns, or elements, and being consequently perplexing and hard to grasp in detail.*

Duress: *Restraint or check by force, stringent compulsion by threat of danger, hardship or retribution.*

Intuition: *It is the act or process of coming to direct knowledge or certainty without reasoning or interfering. Immediate cognizance or conviction without rational thought.*

---

[1] Philip Babcock Gove, Ph. D. Webster's Third New International Dictionary of the English Language Unabridged. Merian Webster Inc. Publishers Springfield, Massachusetts. USA

Albert and Loy Morehead, Philip D. Morehead, The Penguin Webster Handy College Dictionary prepared and edited by the National Lexicographic Board, published by The Penguin Group. New York, NY 10014 USA

David Caroll, the Dictionary of Foreign Terms in The English Language, Hawthorn Books, Inc. publishers/ New York.

Concerting: *It is a union formed by natural communication of opinions and views.*

AFTER WORDS

Retaliate: *To return the like for, to put or inflict in return, make requital (evil for evil).*

Attest: *To bear witness to, affirm to be true or genuine, to authenticate official.*

Intriguing: *Adj. engaging the interest to a marked degree.*

Fury: *It is violent anger, extreme wrath, and unrestrained force.*

CPSIA information can be obtained
at www.ICGtesting.com
Printed in the USA
BVHW04*0959080518
515623BV00003B/18/P